Guard Rails

*10 Vital Questions To Guide
Your Ministry Journey*

❧

TXADOM
Texas Associational Directors
of Missions Network

Guard Rails:
10 Vital Questions To Guide
Your Ministry Journey

Some Scripture quotations are taken from the New American Standard Version of the Bible (NASB) © 1960, 1962, 1963, 1968, 1971, 1972, 1973, 1975, 1977, 1995 by the Lockman Foundation

Some Scripture quotations are taken from the Christian Standard Version of the Bible (CSB) © 2017

Published by
Texas Association of Directors of Missions Network
Printed in the United States of America

Darrell Leon Horn – Editor

Albert Diaz – Cover Design

ISBN 13: 978-0-578-55586-7

To the ministers and churches we serve . . .

2 Corinthians 11:28
*Apart from such external things, there is the
daily pressure on me of concern for all the churches.*

Guard Rails

CONTENTS

1
Introduction
The Value Of Perspective

By Darrell Horn, D. Min.
San Antonio Baptist Association

Another Book?

The other day I sat down on the couch with my computer to work on a document. Because of my eyesight, I always wear a pair of reading glasses anytime I work on the computer. I knew I had picked up my reading glasses but couldn't seem to find them. I walked back to where I had just picked them up and didn't see them. I looked in several other places but still couldn't find them. I thought to myself, "I know I just had them." I became frustrated because I lost them so quickly. Then, I realized my reading glasses were on my nose and I was looking through them all the time. They were right in front of me, but I couldn't see them.

How similar is that example to other areas of our life. Something can be right in front of us, but we either forget it is there or just simply fail to recognize it. God's guard rails for life can be like that.

This book was in its beginning stages before the articles and videos concerning pastoral abuse were published[1] in early February 2019. Such alarming public revelations confirm once again that we need to take a fresh look at sexual abuse committed by Christian leaders. Yet, why another book written on the topic of Christian leaders who disqualify themselves from serving? Good question. Life's journey takes many unexpected turns. Some of those turns are so challenging that if we don't navigate it well, we will severely damage ourselves and those around us. Yes God heals, but many encounters that we face can leave us marked for life. Jacob wrestled with the angel but limped the rest of his life. Such a life experience left its mark on him.

Without guard rails, navigating through the turns on life's road is dangerous. Guard rails are necessary to help us reach our destination in life. We disqualify ourselves from leadership when we overstep certain boundaries. We want to be healthy in all areas of life. We want to the wholistic benefit of having the proper guardrails in place. This book will provide specific guard rails for anyone in leadership positions.

Biblical Models Needed
We are all too aware of many examples, over the past decades, of ministers who have given into temptation and have disqualified themselves from leadership. Leaders in Christ's Church are called to a higher standard of conduct and holiness. Christ demands it. Paul reminded Timothy that *"everyone who names the name of the Lord is to abstain from wickedness."*[2] This book is written with the strongly held belief that the call to holiness among God's people is to be modeled by its leaders. Peter states that leaders are to

---

[1] www.houstonchronicle.com/local/investigations/abuse-of-faith/multimedia.

[2] 2 Timothy 2:19.

shepherd the flock of God among you, exercising oversight not under compulsion, but voluntarily, according to the will of God; and not for sordid gain, but with eagerness; nor yet as lording it over those allotted to your charge, but <u>proving to be examples to the flock</u>.[3]

His words are as applicable today as they were the day, he wrote them.

Years ago, the day before my second graduation from seminary, our President rose to speak in chapel. What he said was something I have remembered and appreciated all these years. He challenged us to remain faithful to God's call on our life and to never disgrace ourselves, our families, the Church and the Lord who had called us. He pleaded with us to leave the ministry before we made decisions, which would disqualify us from serving as a leader in the Church for which Christ died. The same challenge is still needed today.

We are reminded by the inspired words of Peter that *"God has not called us for the purpose of impurity, but in sanctification."*[4] The word sanctification means to set apart as sacred or to consecrate in the service of a sacred purpose. We are set apart by God to live consecrated lives to God. He demands holiness among his people. Peter stated it this way,

> *As obedient children, do not be conformed to the former lusts which were yours in your ignorance, but like the Holy One who called you, be holy yourselves also in all your behavior; because it is written, "You shall be holy, for I am holy.*[5]

---

[3] 1 Peter 5:2-3.
[4] 1 Thessalonians 4:7.
[5] 1 Peter 1:14-16.

A Fresh Call

This book is a renewed call to leaders who are set apart by God and consecrated to God. Holiness must be exemplified among God's leaders. The calling of God to serve Him and His people is a special calling, a divine calling. To violate the standards of such a call is to betray the One who issued that call. Recent news headlines remind us of well-known leaders who were once wonderful examples to follow but ignored important guardrails and disqualified themselves to lead. Our plea to God's leaders includes both current leaders and those whom God will call in the future.

As co-laborers, our appeal, to each of us, is to

> *walk in a manner worthy of the Lord, to please Him in all respects, bearing fruit in every good work and increasing in the knowledge of God; strengthened with all power, according to His glorious might, for the attaining of all steadfastness and patience.*[6]

Let us not disgrace ourselves, our families, the Church and the Lord who had called us. This book is our renewed call to holy living among God's leaders.

Reasons For This Book

The purpose of this book is to propose a series of ten different questions or guard rails related to a leader's journey through life. Each guard rail, that is put and kept in place, will help keep any leader on the road to completing God's call. Ten different Directors, from ten different Texas Associations of churches, will address the ten different guard rails.

---

[6] Colossians 1:10-11.

Firsthand Perspective
What makes this book different is its group of contributors. This book is written from the perspective of network leaders, whose specific ministry calling is to work with other leaders who serve in our local churches.

We, the contributors of this book, serve as Directors[7] of different Associations of churches. We collaborated on this book because we see the need to address the actions by which a leader disqualifies himself. We issue a call to all Christian leaders serving in the local church and to those serving alongside the local church, *"to walk in a manner worthy of the calling with which you have been called."*[8]

This book is written from the perspective of leaders who work closely with ministers, church leaders and churches. Those of us who serve as Directors have a unique perspective. We live in, and are an active part of, the same cities and communities where our churches are located. We too are concerned citizens and residents who share the same interests regarding the welfare of our neighborhoods, local communities, local governments, businesses, and educational systems. We understand firsthand the context in which our churches seek to minister and the challenges they face. We are able to see God at work daily in a local setting as well as understand how to join what He is doing regionally. We can best speak to the issues because we live in the same context as our local churches; where as other leaders who do not reside in our local context but are statewide or national, may not have the same advantage. Paul's statement echoes through our daily activities,

---

[7] This leadership position has been called by many names such as Executive Director, Director of Missions, Associational Missionary and a more recent title of Associational Missions Strategist.
[8] Ephesians 4:1. Other references include Colossians 1:10, 2:6 and 1 Thessalonians 2:12.

"Apart from such external things, there is the daily pressure on me of concern for all the churches."[9] Jeremiah's words, to the children of Israel who were in captivity, help sharpen our focus, *"Seek the welfare of the city where I have sent you into exile and pray to the Lord on its behalf; for in its welfare you will have welfare."[10]*

Close Relationships

The local Association is the closest entity to local churches. Therefore, Directors and their staffs are the closest presence to local churches. We are uniquely focused on serving our churches. Because of our closeness to the local church, we have working relationships with leaders based on trust. Our Associations have existed for many decades. The Association, where I serve, has been in existence for 161 years at the time of this writing. The ongoing relationships between the Association, our churches and church leaders have existed since the founding of each Association.

The value of such long-term relationships is vitally important to continued ministry and cannot be minimized. Directors have private conversations with church leaders every day. A majority of those conversations are highly confidential. We serve in a variety of roles such as friend, confidant, prayer partner, mentor and counselor, to name just a few. Such conversations, which grow out of trusted relationships, are the foundation for healthy Associations and ministries.

Long-term Care

Associational Directors are usually the first ones to deal with the damage from a minister's fall, whatever the reason. We deal with every issue that a church may face. We provide long-term care to many people when a leader disqualifies himself. We see firsthand the damage to the leader, his family, the church

---

[9] 2 Corinthians 11:28.
[10] Jeremiah 29:7.

and the community. Unfortunately, we have seen, more times than we desire, the injury that is left after a leader disqualifies himself from a position of influence. The fallout can be great, and individuals are damaged both directly and indirectly. Such devastation can take many years to heal. God can bring healing and restoration but there is always a scar left behind. No one church or one church leader is an island. Associational Directors and their staff members provide long-term care for churches and leaders.

Need for Guard Rails
We have seen countless examples of ministers who have wrecked, not only their life but, the lives of others, because they either ignored the guard rails or never had them. Guard rails are God's standards for navigating life in the correct lanes on our spiritual pilgrimage through life. At times life's journey can seem like an obstacle course full of potholes, winding curves and oncoming traffic.

Without guard rails, we run the risk of disqualifying ourselves from ministry by not staying in God's designated lanes. Paul reminds us of the importance of living in such a manner, that after we have preached to others, we ourselves will not be disqualified. His words still echo today full of meaning and significance. His letter, inspired by the Spirit of Holiness, to the Church in Corinth, states,

> *Do you not know that those who run in a race all run, but only one receives the prize? Run in such a way that you may win. Everyone who competes in the games, exercises self-control in all things. They then do it to receive a perishable wreath, but we an imperishable. Therefore, I run in such a way, as not without aim; I box in such a way, as not beating the air; but I discipline my body and make it my*

slave, so that, <u>after I have preached to others, I myself will not be disqualified</u>.[11]

May God help us to not disqualify ourselves.

The Importance Of Being Active In An Association Of Churches

The local Association of churches provides a number of opportunities to enhance a leader's ministry and personal spiritual journey. Not only do education and training opportunities exist but also one indispensable needed element in ministry, friends. We need growing friendships with others who are also called into God's service. In our fast-moving society with deadlines and packed schedules, maintaining friendships can be challenging. Yet, it is important for each of us to have a group of other leaders who understand our ministry environment and to hold each other accountable. Our ministry collogues can serve as important guard rails on life's spiritual journey.

In our work as Directors, we understand that every leader will experience difficult times in ministry. Leadership can be a lonely place of responsibility. Leaders at times feel isolated and suffer quietly. We are conditioned to cover up our hurts. Such isolation typically precedes a leader's disqualification. Leaders can help each other by lifting burdens too heavy for one leader to carry.[12]

I recently heard someone comment that in the past he had very few friendships. He concluded that his previous marriage ended

---

[11] 1 Corinthians 9:24-27.

[12] Galatians 6:2. The word *'burden'* used in this verse means a 'burdensome weight'; in order to fulfill the law of Christ, we are called to help each other carry burdens too heavy for one person to carry alone.

in divorce because of not having close friendships with other leaders who could have helped him in a difficult time. His pride and self-confidence contributed to his downfall. Leaders need other leaders for mutual benefit, yet some leaders continue to suffer in silence. Proverbs 27:17 reminds us, *"Iron sharpens iron, so one man sharpens another."*

Here are a few of the many reasons it is important for leaders to be active in an Association of churches.

- Reinforce and clarify God's call on your life
- Stay motivated to fulfill your calling
- Develop regional friendships and connections
- Continuing education and training
- Develop new leadership skills – iron sharpens iron
- Provide laughter and light heartedness
- Offer encouragement and support to lessen ministry stresses
- Provide positive influences to manage negative feelings of self-worth and ministry effectiveness
- Multiply effort in ministry through cooperation
- Stay on the cutting edge of learning
- Learn from another's point of view
- Provide role models and mentors
- Provide accountability partners
- Give back to others
- Provide counsel from co-laborers; In the multitude of counselors there is safety[13]
- Offer collaborative opportunities with leaders

Conclusion

This book is a renewed call to all Christian leaders, to live *"in a manner worthy of the Lord, to please Him in all respects."*[14]

---

[13] Proverbs 11:14.
[14] Colossians 1:10.

Guard Rails

God calls us to place the appropriate guard rails in our lives. The contributing authors of this book offer ten vital questions to help guide us along our spiritual journey in this life. The ten questions cover a wide variety of topics related to who we are as leaders. We desire to be healthy in each area of life.

Each guard rail presented in this book will help us to honorably fulfill the calling of God on our lives. We pray this book will encourage you as much as it did us. May God help us to be *"an example for the believers in speech, in conduct, in love, in faith and in purity."*[15]

---

[15] 1 Timothy 4:12.

2
Who Keeps You Connected?
The Value Of Close Personal Friendships

By Roger A. Yancey, D. Min.
Tryon-Evergreen Baptist Association

As Jim pulled out of the parking lot of the church, he couldn't shake how different the day had started compared to its ending. He had awoken that Wednesday morning with a sense of energy he always felt when he knew his sermon for Sunday was finished and he was even ahead on working on his sermon for the following Sunday as well. The call from Pete Miller, his Chairman of Deacons to get together for coffee at the newest local downtown brew shop would be a chance to find out for himself the rave reviews he had heard about their version of his favorite caffeinated drink, the Cortado.

When Jim entered the Café, he was surprised but glad to see Glenda Wilkins, the Chairperson of Personnel was at the counter ordering a coffee and it appeared she would be joining the conversation as well. It occurred to Jim that this conversation must be about his upcoming 5-year anniversary and perhaps they wanted to run some ideas past him before meeting with the entire Personnel Team. He had mentioned to Glenda several weeks ago that he was not comfortable with having too much of a focus being put on himself but decided to wait and see what they had in mind before trying to minimize their efforts.

After a round of greetings Jim saw Pete fidget in his chair for a bit before clearing his throat and then saying in an unfamiliar tone, "Jim, we need to talk."

The next 45 minutes were both the longest and shortest time periods Jim could ever recall experiencing. His mind reeled with the statements that Pete and Glenda made about his ministry at First Church and the impressions and sentiments they expressed as the appointed voices for both the congregation and his staff.

"Unapproachable" Members were complaining they didn't feel comfortable bringing their concerns directly to him. They expressed earlier attempts resulted in a feeling of being corrected or ignored.

"Unavailable" Members and staff stated Jim was often away from the office and not easily reached when decisions needed to be made or when visits to shut-ins were left undone.

"Unaccountable" The staff in particular felt that Jim was arbitrary in his decision making and favored his own projects over their ministry needs. They saw Jim as drum major of a one-man band and everyone else was expected to march in time with his parade.

"Unconsiderate" Jim knew this wasn't a word but he was too much a preacher to not alliterate. Church members, church leadership and again, his "faithful" (Jim was thinking fitful) staff had shared several ongoing encounters where careless and hurtful words had been spoken by Jim that resulted in wounded hearts. They all expressed that they knew Jim was a "kidder", but the sense of the underlying sarcasm outweighed any humorous value.

Guard Rails

When Pete and Glenda finished talking, they got up to leave while telling Jim to be ready to meet after the Wednesday activities jointly with the Personnel Committee and the Deacon Leadership to determine a way forward so his future ministry could be ensured at First Church. They also directed him to not return to the church office until after they met that night so he wouldn't make the staff uncomfortable as they were all aware of the meeting that morning and the one that evening as well. As Pete said, "Perhaps it would be best for Jim to take a day or two to reflect on what he needed to address before making additional contact with his staff."

When Jim left the downtown area, he found himself driving down one of the many country roads that entwined around the town. His reeling mind ached to find some semblance to the words he had heard versus the life he thought he was experiencing as the pastor of the church. While he could see kernels of truth in many things, they had spoken to him it seemed to be more of a tinker-toy connection of a web of instances instead of an actual reality that was substantive.

He wanted to talk with someone. But who?

Jim knew that if he called his wife Kathy and let her know what had happened that morning she would be devastated. They had just had the staff and their families over to their home a few weeks earlier and nothing seemed amiss. That was part of what was so puzzling and hurtful about this whole thing. Why had no one spoken to him directly?

He knew he needed to talk this out with someone.

Jim's thoughts drifted back to his seminary days more than a decade ago when he would gather each Tuesday at noon with his friends Brent, Chase and Doug. All of them were 2 to 3 years into their first pastorate and they would compare notes, share stories, seek counsel and pray for each other. There was nothing he couldn't share with those guys and those conversations were a source of strength that had got him through some rough patches in his first pastorate and even was a safe place to hurt when he and Kathy had experienced two miscarriages before the birth of their daughter Sarah and later her brother Samuel.

But that was more than 15 years ago, and the circumstances of ministry had caused the drifting away of those close relationships. For a while Brent and Chase had reached out to him but he found it hard to keep up with them. Eventually they quit talking altogether though he would get an email on occasion from Chase who now served as a Director of Missions in a neighboring state.

Life had taken its toll with the pressures Jim experienced as he left seminary to go to a new ministry location 1,000 miles away to start a new church followed by his coming to First Church with its prime location, growing population and his first real fulltime staff to lead. Growth had come and with it the challenge of trying to meet expectations and capture increasing opportunities.

He had a growing ministry with expanding responsibilities in a church that had doubled in attendance since he arrived. But as Jim found himself turning around on a dead-end of a country lane it occurred to him that when he needed a friend the most, he didn't really have anyone that he was comfortable calling.

Oh, he had people he could call but no one other than his wife Kathy who really knew his heart and could be trusted with the pain that was now deeply lodged within it. More out of desperation than desire Jim sent Chase a text asking Chase to let him know when he could call to talk with him.

Jim was surprised when his phone rang within five minutes of sending the text and a voice from the past said, "hello friend, how are you?"

Suddenly Jim felt like he was back at that table in the seminary cafeteria with a cup of coffee in one hand and his heart in the other. Over the next two hours Jim poured out his soul to Chase about the meeting in the coffee shop, his hurt, his frustration and his embarrassment that he had neglected keeping up with their friendship. While Chase shared with Jim many things that would become the foundation of Jim's resetting his ministry footing at First Church there was one concept, he shared with Jim that became foundational in Jim's personal growth as a pastor and a man God could use more fully.

Chase called it the **"Three Circles of Solid Ministry Relationships."** Chase explained that everyone in ministry needed to develop three kinds of relationships so they could navigate and grow in their personal ministry journey. Like the legs of a three-legged stool, each circle was needed for personal stability.

The first circle is the **Ministry Relationships**. Everyone needs to identify and connect with people who are skilled in their ministry vocation that can help us grow in our area of calling. These people are invaluable in helping us understand different and fresh ways of doing ministry, so we continue to be challenged and not get stuck in routine duties. Whether as mentors, coaches or challengers in our lives they drive us forward to be all God called us to be.

The second circle are the **Journey Relationships**. These relationships develop in the journey of our ministry where we connect with people inside and outside of the walls of our church who become important and dear to us. While these relationships can be challenging at times there is a unique strength found in connecting well with our people and loving them even through possible disappointments.

The third circle are the **Heart Relationships**. We need people in our lives who really know our hearts, our joys and our sorrows. Friends who we know without question love us and want the best for our lives. People who see our lives as a reflection of God's glory and have walked with us through the reality of the dark nights of our soul. Friends who can ask us hard questions and speak into our lives truths that cause us to rethink our direction. These are people you can call at 2:00 a.m. and spill out the hurt of your soul without them being more concerned about their losing sleep when you think you're losing your mind.

While this is the smallest circle in number of people in comparison to the other two circles it's the one that can have the strongest impact in shaping us into who we will become.

Chase described the **"Three Circles of Solid Ministry Relationships"** were not separated but often overlapping and interlocking circles of influence in our lives.

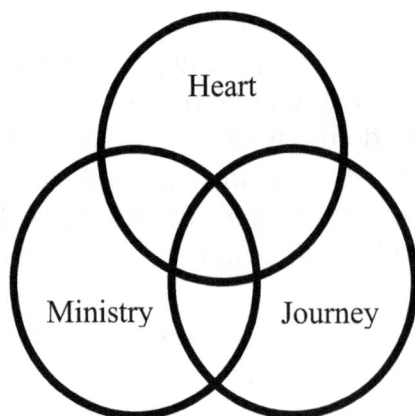

Heart

Ministry   Journey

Chase asked Jim to take time over the next few days and identify people God had put into his life that might fit in each of the three circles and to make note of which circle might be lacking. They agreed they would talk later that week on how he might go about the discovery of who God was putting into the circles of his life.

One thing Jim quickly realized was that he already had someone other than Kathy (his wife and best friend) that he would welcome in his "Heart" circle and he was grateful God had used his moment of challenge to draw him back into his friendship with Chase.

Perhaps like Jim you know what it is to find yourself in a situation where you really need a friend. You may consider yourself to have many "friends" but you don't really have a friend that you can be totally open with without fear of rejection or judgement.

You might have tried to develop those deep friendships in the past and didn't sense it was reciprocated or valued in the same way. Maybe you resonate with the story of the group of ministers who joined a prayer circle and began to share with one another their personal struggles.

"I struggle with gambling" said one, "I struggle with anger" said another, "I struggle with lust" said the one to his side. So summoning his courage the minister shared he struggled with "coarse language" only to hear the final minsiter say, "I struggle with gossip and I have to get out of here and talk to someone."

Whenever we consider Confessional Relationships we must do so within a construct of wisdom and discernment but to fail to develop them is to position yourself to experience the reality of Proverbs 16:18 *"Pride goes before destruction and a haughty spirit before a fall."*

So what do you do now? How do you ensure that you don't live out your minsitry in self imposed isolation?

Guard Rails

Consider taking the following steps as a beginning point.

1. Prayerfully list your three circles and identify who God has brought into you life in each area. You might find in the Ministry Circle that you want to consider just including your top 10 instead of listing everyone possible. Limit your list to those who are ready to invest in you and help you grow in your minstry. Do the same for your Journey Circle and finally your Heart Circle.

2. Identify where the gaps are in each circle – which circle is lacking (or absent) of people who would make up the circle.

3. Began to pray specifically for God to add people to your **"Three Circles of Solid Ministry Relationships"** as he sees fit. Remember, friends are made they don't just appear.

4. Ask yourself where you might fit in the circles of someone elses life. Is there someone who is trying to connect with you that you haven't made time for? Are you open to God planting you in someone else's life just as you need to have others planted into yours?

Resources

David Dusek. *Rough Cut Men: A Man's Battle Guide to Building Real Relationships with Each Other, and with Jesus.* Grace Publishing. 2015.

Patrick Morley. *The Man in the Mirror: Solving the 24 Problems Men Face.* Zondervan. 2014.

Jonathan Holmes. *The Company We Keep: In Search of Biblical Friendship.* Cruciform Press. 2014.

Gordon McDonald. *Ordering Your Private World.* Thomas Nelson. 2015.

Guard Rails

3
Who Asks The Hard Questions?
The Value Of Laser Focused Conversations

By Tom Henderson, Ph.D.
Bell Baptist Association

What Is It?

"Brother Henderson, will you help some ministers in your area counsel with another minister who has been fired by his church for immorality?" I was stunned by the question. I had heard there were some problems in the church where the fired pastor had served, but was unaware of the depth or severity of the issues. I gathered the concerned ministers together and began a year long journey to restore a minister who had crashed through several important guard rails. Through that painful time, I learned that ministers need people in their lives who at regular intervals are asking the hard questions of an accountability partner with the goal of preventing ministerial crashes.

Accountability according to Merriam Webster means, "An obligation or willingness to accept responsibility or to account for one's actions."[1] We are all accountable in a variety of

---

[1] Merriam-Webster Dictionary. Merriam-Webster Publisher. 2016.

relationships. According to the author of the website, AllAboutGOD.com,

> The Bible says that God holds us accountable. Romans 14:12 says, "So then each of us shall give account of himself to God." This is personal accountability. Christians are also accountable to one another. In 1 Corinthians chapter 12, we read that Christians are all part of the same body - the body of Christ - and each member needs or belongs to the other. This Scripture suggests the importance of strong accountability between Believers. It is important for every Believer to have at least one other person in which to confide, pray with, listen to, and encourage. Galatians 6:1-2 gives a helpful principle, "Brothers, if someone is caught in a sin, you who are spiritual should restore him gently. But watch yourself, or you also may be tempted. Carry each other's burdens, and in this way you will fulfill the law of Christ." If your accountability friend has done something contrary to the Bible, you are called to confront him gently, forgive him, and comfort him. It also admonishes you to consider yourself because no one is above temptation. Another aspect of Christian accountability is encouraging each other to grow in their spiritual maturity. Hebrews 10:24 says, "And let us consider how we may spur one another on toward love and good deeds." 1 Thessalonians 5:11 says to, "...encourage one another and build each other up... [2]

Richard J. Krejcir with Schaeffer Institute of Church Leadership says of Christian Accountability:

> Accountability allows us to be answerable to one another, with the focus on improving our key relationships with people such as our spouse, close friends, colleagues, coworkers, a boss, small group members, or a pastor.

---

[2] www.allaboutgod.com/christian-accountability.html.

Accountability will also enhance our integrity, maturity, character relationships in general, and our growth in Christ. Accountability is sharing, in confidence, our heartfelt Christian sojourn in an atmosphere of trust so we can give an answer for what we do, see where we need help, understand our struggles and where we are weak, and be encouraged to stay on track, seek prayer, care, and support when we fail, and model guideposts for one another to keep us going.[3]

Accountability is achieved when the individuals in a group take responsible for their actions.

Do We Need It?

Most ministers I talk to express a need for accountability, but do not take the initiative or spend the time and energy necessary to be accountable. Too often ministers think in terms of crisis management rather than preventative maintenance. They generally will rally to respond to a broken situation to help someone else, but seldom will they call upon others to help them place or maintain guard rails of accountability in their own lives.

Chuck Lawless, Dean of Doctoral Studies and Vice-President of the Spiritual Formation and Ministry Centers at Southeastern Seminary in Wake Forest, NC, has given eight reasons why every church leader needs accountability partner(s): [4]

1. It's biblical. It is through the help of another, like iron sharpening iron, that we grow. (Prov. 27:17). We are to

---

[3]www.intothyword.org/apps/articles/default.asp?blogid=0&view=post&articleid=32244&link=1&fldKeywords=&fldAuthor=&fldTopic=0.
[4]www.chucklawless.com/2017/05/8-reasons-every-church-leader-needs-accountability.

challenge each other to live in godliness (Heb. 3:12-13), confronting one another when necessary (Matt. 18:15-17, Luke 17:3). We are to carry one another's burdens, including provoking each other to good works (Both thoughts are not in this verse)(Heb. 10:24) and picking each other up when we fall (Gal. 6:1-2). (The first appendix gives other Biblical references.) what book does this refer to? definitely needs footnote(s).

2. We are all prone to wander. As soon as we think that we've "arrived" in our faithfulness to God, we've just fallen farther away. One problem is that we often don't recognize sin in ourselves.

3. We're in spiritual warfare. The principalities and powers identified in Ephesians 6:12 particularly aim their arrows at church leaders on the front lines of the battle against evil. Satan and his forces find us most vulnerable when we minister alone, with no one walking beside us and provoking us to good works (Heb. 10:24).

4. Leaders often hide their sin. Because we're leaders, we don't typically want others to know what's going on in the depth s of our soul – but that's exactly where the demons lurk when no one else has access to our heart. (choose one or the other: heart or soul?)

5. We commit flagrant sins of omission. Too many church leaders are tempted and teach a Bible they seldom read, call others to pray like they seldom do, and preach evangelism they never exhibit. We need somebody who asks us hard questions about this discrepancies.

6. Our congregations need models. We minister to people who are themselves struggling with sin, and we encourage them to find an accountability partner to help them. To call others to take this step when we don't, lacks integrity.

7. It forces us to swallow our pride. Most of us church leaders could use a little more humility, and few things break us like looking a friend in the eye and admitting our sin issues.

8. We're more likely to end well with accountability in place. Having an accountability partner doesn't guarantee lifelong faithfulness, but it at least makes falling more difficult.

Lawless' comments call leaders to account for their faithfulness and that of those around them. Perhaps we would be more adamant about accountability if we took to heart the sobering words of Dietrich Bonhoeffer as shared by Kris Dolberry, on the LIFEWAY MEN Webb Site blogs,

> Sin demands to have a man by himself. It withdraws him from the community. The more isolated a person is, the more destructive will be the power of sin over him, and the more deeply he becomes involved in it, the more disastrous is his isolation.[5]

How To Do It?

There are many ways to have an accountability partner or group. They range from the use of professional counselors for major disruptions in life, to simply having a personal quiet time with the LORD in your daily devotions. For the purpose of this chapter, we will examine the guard rail of accountability as applied through small intimate groups that use a specific set of questions.

According to the author of the website, AllAboutGOD.com, small intimate groups are effective in accountability when trust is present. Trust is the glue that keeps the group together and on task. The author shares that trust is developed when there is active listening (James 1:19), non-judgmental attitudes

---

[5] blog.lifeway.com/leadingmen/2016/03/02/accountability.

(Matthew 7:1-2), and deep caring for one another (I John 4:21). He sums by saying, "Accountability involves a willingness to open yourself up and share sensitive or personal information. This is why trust is so imperative. If you sense trust, you are more open to share your innermost thoughts without concern of betrayal."[6]

The second aspect of this guard rail is having specific questions for the group to use. The questions used need to be general enough to gauge a person's actions and pointed enough to hold him accountable to God, Himself, and others. Questions should be unique to the group and the needs of its members. I found many lists of accountability questions are available for reference ranging in length from two questions to 58 questions.

Kris Dolberry who leads Ministry to Men at LifeWay Resources.com and also serves as Executive Editor of Stand Firm, a daily devotional magazine for men, suggests the following general list of questions to be used in an accountability group as it begins:[7]

1. Have you spent daily time in God's Word and in prayer?

2. Have you flirted, or had lustful attitudes, tempting thoughts, or exposed yourself to any explicit materials which would not glorify God?

3. Have you been completely above reproach in your financial dealings?

4. Have you pursued the hearts of your wife and kids?

5. Have you done your 100% best in your job, school, etc.?

---

[6] www.allaboutgod.com/christian-accountability.html.
[7] blog.lifeway.com/leadingmen/2016/03/02/accountability.

6. Have you told any half-truths or outright lies, putting yourself in a better light to those around you?

7. Have you shared the Gospel with an unbeliever this week?

8. Have you taken care of your body through daily physical exercise and proper eating/sleeping habits?

9. Have you allowed any person or circumstance to rob you of your joy?

10. Have you lied on any of your answers?

What Should It Look Like?

The use of an intimate group and specific questions has historical precedence with the Holy Club at Oxford University in 1729. John and Charles Wesley got together with a handful of other Oxford students devoted themselves to a rigorous search for holiness and service to others. Christian researcher and writer, Ed Stetzer lists 21 questions that the group used.[8] This group was never a large group, but the participants went on to become great leaders in the Christian work of the day. A list of the members and their contributions have been complied by *Christian History*.[9]

Chris Easley, reporting in *Christianity Today,* shares the characteristics of a successful accountability group.[10]

---

[8] Ed Stetzer. "Accountability Questions." *Christianity Today.* May 5, 2008.
[9] John Wesley. *Christian History.* Issue 2: "John Wesley: Leader of the Methodist Movement." "The Holy Club." 1983.
[10] Chris Easley. *How To Start An Accountability Group.* Christianitytoday.com. October 4, 2006.

Guard Rails

1. Vulnerability. Each member is honest about how he has failed.

2. Accepting of God's Love and Forgiveness. Each member accepts God's forgiveness for his sin, trusting him and rejecting feelings of guilt and shame.

3. Validation and Support. Regardless of what temptations a member struggles with or how he has sinned, he should be accepted by the group and loved, not judged or ridiculed.

4. Trust and Safety. What is shared in the group stays in the group.

5. Prayer. The members of the group together ask God to help them with their specific struggles, strengthen them as they face temptation, forgive them when they fail, and help them stand up again to walk with him and live as "more than conquerors through him."[11]

6. Accountability. If a member is struggling with a certain sin or temptation and shares this with the group, the group will hold him or her accountable to act in a godly way in that area.

7. Ownership. Each member that participates in the group is consciously engaged in the group's meetings.

8. Fellowship and Friendship. All of the members build healthy friendships with each other as brothers and sisters in Christ.

Members of an Accountability Group ask each other the tough questions and expect others to give honest and complete answers.

---

[11] Ibid.

How To Begin?

There are several key steps to implement this guardrail of Accountability.

1. Prayer is the first step. The prayer will have several components. First there must be an attitude of personal humility and commitment to the process of becoming accountable to others. Next comes a request for clarity about which specific areas of accountability the group will limit itself to and focus on. The final prayer component is asking for discernment when selecting members to join the group.

2. Enlist group members. During conversations, ask if there is interest in an accountability group.

3. In a group information meeting, explain accountability and what would be involved in joining this group. Present a proposed schedule and agenda for meetings. Finally hand out the proposed covenant, including the values listed by Leslie Bennett.[12] Set a deadline for the potential group members commit to join.

4. Gather the members and discuss the guidelines for the new group. Gather the signed covenants and, offer a prayer of commitment for each person in the new Accountability Group.

---

[12] Leslie Bennett. *Accountability Group Covenant.* www.ReviveOurHearts.com.

Resources

The following pdf link provides accountability questions from multiple sources, such as:

- www.clevedonbaptistchurch.org/wp-content/uploads/2013/06/Accountability-Questions1.pdf
- John Wesley's Small Group
- Wesley's Band Meeting
- Chuck Swindoll's Pastoral Accountability
- Renovare: James Bryan Smith and Richard Foster
- Phil Helfer, Los Alto Brethren Church in Long Beach, CA
- Highway Community in Palo Alto, CA
- Florent Varak of Lyon
- H. Neil Cole
- Dave Guiles, director of Grace Brethren International Missions
- Paul Klawitter of France

4
Where Do You Find Happiness?
The Value Of True Contentment

By David Bowman, D. Min.
Tarrant Baptist Association

My Experience

Father of the Bride in black and white with Spencer Tracy and Elizabeth Taylor, and the remake with Steve Martin, are great movies. They do not reflect my family's reality at all.

For my daughter's wedding, I ran errands, my wife Katie, the CPA and Associate Superintendent for Finance and Auxiliary Operations, handled the financial end of things and our Baby Girl stretched the budget to the breaking point.

Paula, my daughter, and I have been preparing for her wedding day since she was a little girl. Everywhere we went, she placed her hand in the crook of my arm as we walked together. There is no telling how many miles we have journeyed like that. Those are great memories.

I also remember when Paula was baptized as a child. She trusted Christ as an eight-year-old. Her mother and I spent several weeks making sure she understood her commitment.

Guard Rails

Then we gathered family and friends for the big day. We stood around the baptistry laughing and telling stories. Seconds before the stained-glass window covering the baptistry was removed, Paula closed her eyes, slightly bowed her head, and raised her hands to shush us all. It was time to begin.

In recent years, we have still taken long walks together around Fort Worth. We talked and prayed and laughed and cried. I loved those walks.

More recently, she has been walking with Connor, her fiancé/husband, and their curly puppy, Indie. But last week, we took the walk we have thought about and dreamed of and planned for a long time. The wedding rehearsal went well. Everyone knew their places and responsibilities. On the big day, our son, Jonathan, led the groomsmen into their places and he stood at the front to receive us. The bridesmaids stood evenly spaced on the stairs leading down into the main hall. A last-minute change required precise movements to hit our spots at the right time. One bridesmaid turned to Paula and asked, "Now? "Paula closed her eyes, slightly bowed her head, raised her hands, and said, "Now."

Moments later, as we descended the stairs, people stood and smiled, and we walked together again just as we had rehearsed for so many years with her hand in the crook of my arm. Some walks are far too short.

What came next was simple and straightforward. It was one of the highlights of my life. I had arrived at the place in the service where I said, "Connor, you may kiss my Baby Girl!" With that, they became husband and wife.

There were many steps leading me and my family to where we are today. Around a quarter of a century ago, I served in a growing church with all the challenges involved. I was also working on the Doctor of Ministry degree. My son Jonathan had started school. Paula was still a toddler. Truth be told, I was overwhelmed with all the responsibilities.

Every time I attended chapel at Southwestern Baptist Theological Seminary, the guest speaker was introduced as The World's Foremost Expert in Something or Other. I wondered what I would ever become the world's foremost expert in.

I discovered what I was to become an expert in while lying face down in the carpet and crying my eyes out. Taking care of my wife and children, navigating a church through growing pains, and staying up late every night to read and write took a toll. The price was high. Through those tears and out of that anguish came a resolve to become The World's Foremost Expert in My Wife and Kids. I decided not to allow anyone to know them better than me. I would learn to love what they loved and to participate in their favorite activities with them.

I drove them to school in the mornings and picked them up in the afternoon as often as possible. I learned to listen so that they would talk. I discovered that a well-placed and well-timed open-ended question stimulated conversation better than: "How was your day?"

We learned together, we played together, we laughed together. We shared movies and books and television shows. We learned to think together and to celebrate moments large and small.

When we moved to our present location, my wife wanted to finish her MBA which was delayed years before by another move and another birth. My job was to research the local and online options. We found the right program at the right price. For the next two years, she spent Monday evenings and Saturday mornings in class. She graduated with a perfect 4.0. She was named a University Scholar.

Guard Rails

Our son Jonathan and some of his peers decided after 9/11, 2001, that they were going to join the military as soon as they were old enough. They were then only in the eighth grade. Later one attended the Naval Academy and serves as a Navy fighter pilot, two brothers enlisted right out of high school, one joined the Army, the other joined the Marines, and one young man joined the Texas National Guard.

To help Jonathan prepare for his military service, he began a reading program we designed together. He read about military leaders of ancient history and those of more current campaigns. He learned about the challenges and sacrifices of such a life. He wrestled with the consequences of battle. Jonathan chose college rather than enlisting. His choices were the United States Military Academy, The Naval Academy, and Texas A&M. We researched each option. As soon as he received his acceptance letter from Texas A&M, he closed the other files.

After Paula's junior year of high school, she and her mother went to Guatemala with Buckner International. They worked in orphanages. It broke Paula's heart to see so many children who would never enjoy the good life she had. She decided she was going to go to college as a Political Science major, then attend law school, and then protect the little ones.

She followed her dream and recently became an Assistant District Attorney. She wants to move up through the system to the Special Victims Unit where she will protect the little ones.

Our daughter-in-law Erica is well on her way to becoming The World's Foremost Expert in Jonathan. Our son-in-law Connor is becoming The World's Foremost Expert in Paula. When they arrive, I will celebrate with them and the completion of a large part of my life mission which continues with my wife. No person will ever beat me out in this regard concerning Katie. It is fun continuing to learn her intricacies after all these years. Walking and talking, playing and praying together with those I love most is where I encounter my greatest happiness, my deepest contentment.

How To Build A Contented Life

Make The Most Of What You Have
"I know both how to make do with little, and I know how to make do with a lot. In any and all circumstances I have learned the secret of being content – whether well fed or hungry, whether in abundance or in need. I am able to do all things through him who strengthens me."[1]

Enjoy What You Have
Get the full benefit of whatever God places in your hands. I remember my grandmother, who grew up in the Great Depression, saying people used everything on a hog except the squeal.

Get The Best Bang For The Buck On Everything
"Keep your life free from the love of money. Be satisfied with what you have, for he himself has said, I will never leave you or abandon you."[2]

Neither A Hoarder Nor A Spend-Thrift Be
Instead, find the most value for your means. If the best car you can afford is a ten-year-old third-hand pickup, drive it with pride! If you can afford something really nice, choose to maximize safety and style.

---

[1] Philippians 4:12-13.
[2] Hebrews 13:5.

Guard Rails

Delight In Dinnertime -
Even If All You Have Is A Salad Or Brussels Sprouts
"But godliness with contentment is great gain. For we brought nothing into the world, and we can take nothing out. If we have food and clothing, we will be content with these."[3]

I could enjoy a balanced diet of steak, lobster, pizza, and Mexican food for daily dinners. However, there have been times when all we could afford to eat was what we grew in the garden and whatever was cheapest at the grocery store. I enjoy wearing nice clothes and looking good. I was Best Dressed Boy in the eighth grade in the fine fashions my mother bought for me at Sears.

Turn Worries Into Prayers
"Don't worry about anything, but in everything, through prayer and petition with thanksgiving, present your requests to God."[4]

Where God guides, He provides. If He has not provided it, ask him for it. What concerns cause you anxiety? What fears prevent your forward progress? Turn those issues into prayers.

Treasure What Matters Most
This life has taken me many places into adventures of all kinds. Traveling to distant places real to me previously only through written and visual media is often thrilling. However, my favorite place in the world is wherever my family is. I love our little Hobbit hole on the side of the hill. I delight in our dinners together. I love our long walks.

---

[3] 1 Timothy 6:6-8.
[4] Philippians 4:6.

One Final Thought

I will finish my life with as few regrets as possible related to missing meaningful moments together. I am completely content with missing anything and everything which takes me away from my role as World's Foremost Expert in My Wife and Kids. That's where I find my contentment.

Guard Rails

Resources

Ron Blue and Karen Guess. *Never Enough? 3 Keys to Financial Contentment*. B&H Books. 2017.

Rachel Cruze. *Love Your Life, Not Theirs*. Ramsey Press. 2016.

Richard Foster. *Freedom of Simplicity*. HarperOne. 2005.

Dallas Willard. *Life Without Lack*. Thomas Nelson. 2019.

5
What Makes You Feel Complete?
The Value Of Understanding God's Design

By Ernie McCoulskey, M. Div.
Kauf Van Baptist Association

All people in ministry will experience times of deep inner joy and fulfillment. It is the best part of the journey. They will also encounter darker times feeling dissatisfied or even defeated. One feeling does not make a person a success any more than the other feeling makes a person a failure. Having the self-awareness to understand from where such feelings may come is important to safeguard a person's ministry.

Reggie McNeal expresses the need for self-awareness this way:

> Leaders who operate without self-awareness run the risk of being blindsided by destructive impulses and confused by emotions that threaten to derail their agenda and leadership effectiveness. . . . In short, leaders lacking self-awareness are besieged from within. They are often their own worst enemy.[1]

---

[1] Reggie McNeal. *Practicing Greatness: Seven Disciplines of Extraordinary Spiritual Leaders*. Jossey-Bass. 2006. Pg. 11.

Our Uniqueness

All of us are made in the image of God. Within that image He has also made each of us unique. Coming to understand our own uniqueness is a journey, but it is a journey worth taking. We were all created physically, emotionally and spiritually different from each other.

Many ministers beginning their ministry journey have in their minds a model of what a "great pastor" should look like. That model almost always looks like someone of great influence from their past. That model may have been a pastor that they admired or someone who personally mentored them along the way. Or, it may have been a family member, a famous evangelist, or an influential professor. To ministers who look to someone past or present to be their model, I have only two words: STOP IT! Don't compromise your uniqueness.

In this chapter we will first examine God-given differences, then we will consider four basic introspective questions. Always keep in mind that although we are all different from one another, each of us was made by the Father and in His image.

What Are Your Spiritual Gifts?

Almost all Christians agree that every follower of Christ is gifted in some way to further His Kingdom. We do not all have the same gifts. Spiritual gifts are not of themselves a sign of spiritual maturity or success. All gifts are important for the church. That is about where the agreement ends.

The New Testament has three primary lists of spiritual gifts, Romans 12:3-8, I Corinthians 12:7-11 and Ephesians 4:11. If needed, there are several man-made spiritual gift discovery tools to help identify a person's gifts. If you have never used one, I would encourage you to do so, but I would warn you to stay away from surveys that ask only 10-12 questions.

Currently my favorite tool to help someone seeking to discover their giftedness is provided free of charge on the Denison Forum website. It has approximately 90 diagnostic questions with 5 possible answers for each question and it is self-graded. Results are given almost immediately. No tool is perfect, and it is not to take the place of the Holy Spirit's leading, but this can be a helpful tool.

I want to give a personal warning to pastors who might use a man-made tool to determine spiritual giftedness. Many outstanding preachers that I know do not have preaching as their primary gift. That's OK. When I first took an inventory years ago and found out my primary spiritual gifts were identified as encouragement and hospitality, I was deeply disappointed. As I matured and embraced my giftedness, I discovered that my gifts of encouraging people and making them feel comfortable actually enriched my preaching. As you discover and embrace your unique giftedness, trust that God gave you gifts that can enrich your preaching as well.

What Is Your Relational Style?

How people relate to others, how they relate to their surroundings and how they react when under stress are important things to know. Understanding those things about yourself and those closest to you is even more important.

As far back as ancient Greece, personality differences were observed and categorized. They seemed to naturally fall into four main categories. While modern social science recognizes that personality and relational style are far more complex, there is still great value in learning the four basic styles and identifying which most closely fits you.

Different sources use different terms. The chart below may help keep the terminologies in line.

Description	DISC[2]	Smalley/Trent[3]	LaHaye[4]
Dominant	D	Lion	Choleric
Influencing	I	Otter	Sanguine
Steadiness	S	Golden Retriever	Phlegmatic
Conscientious	C	Beaver	Melancholic

I will use the DISC terminology to describe the four personality types because I am most familiar with it. After all, I am an "S" and I would hate to call myself "Phlegmatic" because some people might think I have a lung condition.

"D" – Dominant folks love well defined goals and the active pursuit of achieving them. They are project oriented. On a mixed team, they will tend to try to keep the team "on task". They may not be in charge, but there is a part of them that wants to be. They like change and dislike the routine. These folks need to be careful not to become too controlling and may even be viewed as manipulative by others.

"I" – Influencers love to talk. They work great in teams that have a friendly and fun environment. On a mixed team, they tend to bring enthusiasm and flexibility to the task. They need to be careful to stay on task and follow through to completion.

"S" – Steady folks love working together. They are consensus builders and are supportive of the group. On a mixed team, they bring a sense of deliberate cooperation. They need to be careful

---

[2] www.discprofile.com/what-is-disc/overview.
[3] www.dbu.edu/jeanhumphreys/SocialPsych/smalleytrentpersonality.html.
[4] www.joydigitalmag.com/everyday-life/the-4-spirit-controlled-temperaments.

because they dislike confrontation and change. They can become too compromising in order to avoid confrontation.

"**C**" – Conscientious folks see the details and want them to be correct. They tend to be very conscientious about the task at hand. In a mixed group, they act either officially or unofficially as a quality control presence. They need to be careful not to become hard and inflexible. At times, their need to have all the details can lead to indecisiveness.

Did you notice that every personality type has both great strengths and potential weaknesses? There is not a right type or a wrong type. Each type can act as a team leader or member. It is especially important for the team leader to be not only aware of his own personality but also of those that he leads. I believe great teams are made up of a mixture of all four types.

There are more advanced tools to help you identify relational styles in greater detail. The *Myers-Briggs Type Indicator*[5] divides the four general groups in sixteen sub-groups; however, using the inventories that deal with only four main personality types is sufficient to start your journey of self-discovery in this area

One of my favorite tools for identifying someone's personality type, which uses the DISC tool, is C. Gene Wilkes' study entitled JESUS ON LEADERSHIP: Becoming A Servant Leader.[6] You can purchase it in a five-week workbook format from Lifeway Christian Resources. It includes not only the DISC inventory but a spiritual gifts inventory as well.

---

[5] www.myersbriggs.org/my-mbti-personality-type/mbti-basics
[6] C. Gene Wilks. *Jesus on Leadership: Becoming a Servant Leader*. LifeWay. 2015.

Are You A Social Or A Solitary Person?

I grew up in a very gregarious or social family. While my personality certainly would measure high on an extrovert scale, my friends laugh at me when I tell them that I am the quiet one in my family. Since my mentors in ministry were also all extroverts to some degree or another, I assumed all ministers were extroverts. Boy was I wrong.

As I have become acquainted with more and more pastors over time, I have met many outstanding pastors that I would identify as introverted or solitary personality types. Dr. Thom Rainer has done introverted ministers a great service by writing widely about his experiences as a very successful introverted leader, both in the church and as President of LifeWay Christian Resources.

While every pastor is completely unique, I have come up with a few general observations relating to social and solitary personalities in the ministry.

1. The role of today's pastor contains both a social part and a solitary part.

2. The "successful" extroverted pastor will bond with his people out of his passion. He is a shepherding pastor by nature. He wants to be wanted and needs to be needed. He loves his people and they know it. But there is another side to ministry. The extroverted pastor must also spend hours every week in solitude praying, studying and preparing sermons. Because he loves the Lord and his Word, at times he must discipline himself to stay in solitude and complete those tasks.

3. The "successful" introverted pastor's passion is to be alone in his study. If he could, he could spend almost all his time alone with the Lord. He wants to be meticulously prepared

to preach on Sunday. He prays in his solitude. But there is another side of ministry and he must discipline himself to spend time with people, both church people and lost people. At times he must be reminded that people don't care how much you know until they know how much you care. He too must adjust his schedule because of his love for the Lord and His people.

Are You Divinely Called?

Here is the bottom line! Has God called you to church work? If you are certain of this then you must keep learning and growing in self-awareness. This knowledge will help safeguard your ministry. God made you unique. He gave you spiritual gifts. He gave you a relational style and personality type. You may need to learn to be more introverted or extroverted. God knew all of that when He invited you to join Him in His work.

Conclusion

Becoming more self-aware has many benefits for the minister. Being aware of your uniqueness provides an important guardrail to protect your ministry from Satan's attacks when he tries to demean you or lead you into over-confidence. Knowing your spiritual gifts and personality style can help you navigate through challenging times in ministry. An added benefit is being able to anticipate and understand the responses you get from persons with certain identifiable gifts and/or personality traits. This is a great asset in leading teams in the church. Understanding yourself and others can greatly enhance your personal life and ministry.

Resources

C. Gene Wilkes. *Jesus on Leadership: Becoming a Servant Leader*. LifeWay Christian Resources. 2015.

Reggie McNeal. *Practicing Greatness: Seven Disciplines of Spiritual Leaders.* A Leadership Network Publication, Jossey-Bass. 2006.

Jim Denison. The Denison Forum. Online resource, denisonforum.org.

Paul David Tripp. *Dangerous Calling*. Crossway Books. 2012.

Smalley Institute. *Personality Test.*
www.accounseling.org/wp-content/uploads/2018/10/
Personality-Test-Smalley.pdf

6
What Makes You Tick?
The Value Of Being Conformed To Christ's Image

By John Thielepape, D. Min.
Parker Baptist Association

In the first lines of his classic book on spiritual disciplines Richard Foster wrote, "Superficiality is the curse of our age. The desperate need today is not for a greater number of intelligent people, or gifted people, but for deep people." *The Celebration of Discipline* was first published in 1978, but the words remain potent more than forty years later.[1]

When we consider the inner spiritual life as a guardrail for ministry, superficiality remains a tempting shortcut. Busy schedules, demanding parishioners, unclear expectations, competing priorities, and personal doubts will pull ministers in different directions. Activity can masquerade for spiritual vitality, and the relationship depth with Jesus that is required to nurture the soul can become shallow.

---

[1] Richard J. Foster. *Celebration of Discipline: The Path to Spiritual Growth, Revised Edition*. San Francisco: Harper San Francisco. 1988. Pg. 1.

Instead of being continuously replenishing, the spiritual well can to run dry. But like everyone else, ministers continue to be invited by Jesus to: "Remain in me, and I in you. Just as a branch is unable to produce fruit by itself unless it remains on the vine, neither can you unless you remain in me."[2]

The guardrail of the inner life can be represented by a healthy relationship with God demonstrated by a growing faith, dependence upon Jesus, and consistent character.

Growing Faith

Churches often look at ministers with the belief that they are spiritually complete, and have little or no expectation for the minister's continued growth. In fact, some church members do not want to know that their ministers are still subject to spiritual growth, fight temptation, or that they ever struggle with obedience. Since ministers are looked upon as the "spiritual experts" and sometimes as "spiritual celebrities," the need to nurture a continually growing faith can be ignored by congregations and ministers alike.

Spiritual vitality requires growing faith; defined as the increasing ability to give our deepest trust and loyalty to God resulting in a richer sense of meaning and purpose centered upon that relationship. Growing Christian faith means breaking the attachments that lead us away from God and developing the attachments that draw us closer to him.

James Fowler developed the *Stage Theory of Faith Development* as a way to outline a series of stages that describe the developing pattern by which the trust and loyalty of faith are demonstrated and bring meaning and purpose to the Christian life. Patterns of trust develop as one confronts the challenges and turning points of life. These challenges allow the

---

[2] John 15:4.

opportunity to move into new levels of understanding and dependence on God's faithfulness.[3]

Effective ministry requires ministers to be honest about how the challenges they confront invite them into a larger and richer understanding of how God wants to work in their lives. The guardrail of the inner life will be strengthened when ministers acknowledge that, like Paul, we must continue to grow. *"Not that I have already reached the goal or am already perfect, but I make every effort to take hold of it because I also have been taken hold of by Christ Jesus."*[4]

Dependence Upon Jesus

Ministers work best when their service flows from a deep relationship with Jesus. They cannot bear spiritual fruit without abiding in him. Christ abides in the believer and the believer abides in him. This spiritual vitality produces obedience and fruit, as well as meaning and spiritual abundance in the believer's life.

The Apostle Paul uses the formula "in Christ" 164 times in the New Testament and the phrase expresses how being located within the sphere of Christ's influence has an impact upon a believer's life.[5] Boyd Hunt writes that "the phrase *in Christ* expresses the limitless resources for redemption that God

---

[3] James W. Fowler, *Becoming Adult, Becoming Christian: Adult Development and Christian Faith*. San Francisco: Harper San Francisco. 1984. Pgs. 74-75.

[4] Philippians 3:12

[5] Adolf Deissmann, trans. By William E. Wilson. *Paul: A Study in Social and Religious History*. New York: Harper & Brothers Publishers. 1957. Pg. 140.

provides through Christ."[6] Being positioned in Christ as a result of salvation received by grace through faith[7] and turning toward him in obedience leads to consistently abiding in him in a way that produces spiritual fruit.

What does spiritual superficiality look like in a minister's life? Superficiality demonstrates itself in attitudes and behaviors that indicate dependence upon self rather than upon Jesus.

Mike Breen uses the temptations of Jesus as a framework to describe the traps that can pull us back from abiding in Christ. He describes them as the temptations of appetite, ambition and approval. Each of these traps exist on its own continuum. Drifting off center to the extremes of the continuum can create a subtle drift from spiritual vitality.[8]

For ministers, the continuum of appetite is represented by the extremes of need and satisfaction. On one end, ministers never seem to have enough resources (time, people, money, programs) to be effective, and a scarcity mindset influences their decisions. They can develop a habit of making excuses and either fail to trust in God's provision or convince themselves that God can provide for them in only one way.

On the other end of the appetite continuum, satisfaction can cause ministers to lose their sense of dependence upon Jesus for continued growth and drift from spiritual vitality. Success might convince them that they possess the talent, resources, and

---

[6] Boyd Hunt. *Redeemed! Eschatological Redemption and the Kingdom of God*. Nashville: Broadman & Holman Publishers. 1993. Pg. 145.
[7] Ephesians 2:8-9.
[8] Mike Breen. *Building a Discipling Culture: How to Release a Missional Movement by Discipling People Like Jesus Did*. Greenville: 3DM Publishing. 2017. Pgs. 60-69.

power to accomplish what they want and to place their trust in their own abilities.

The second drift, ambition, pulls between the extremes of strength and weakness. On one hand, ministers are driven by accomplishment and evaluate their ministries based upon what they can achieve. This can lead to evaluating other people based upon how much they help the minister achieve his own goals.

On the other extreme of the ambition continuum, ministers focus upon their weaknesses and use them as excuses for a lack of accomplishment. Instead of allowing their weaknesses to be an opportunity for Jesus to demonstrate his glory, they become the justifications used for failing to realize their ambitions. Or worse, ministers may focus upon the weaknesses of others and blame them for failures.

The third drift, approval, swings on its continuum between acceptance and rejection. One extreme of this drift results in believing that ministers are superior to the people they are supposed to serve. Instead of seeing them as people to love and serve, they become the tools at our disposal for success or self-acceptance. Instead of leading them to serve Jesus, we lead them to serve us to feed our need for acceptance.

On the opposite extreme of the continuum: rejection, the minister experiences the constant pressure to please others. Ministers can let criticisms and the unreasonable expectations of others take control, and spend their time trying to live up to what others want. In doing so, they often fail to protect their families. They live with the constant and impossible to satisfy expectation to make other people happy. Eventually, this can lead to disillusionment and depression.

Each person swings along these continuums in varying degrees on a weekly basis. On one extreme, a minister can trust too much in his own resources, successes and capabilities. On the other extreme ministers can live in scarcity, believing that they do not have what it takes to be successful and become paralyzed by the fear of failure.[9]

The center point, where ministers can achieve balance in each continuum, is to trust in Jesus, be constantly aware of their need for him and believe in the sufficiency of his provision. Then they can understand the secret of contentment that Paul described in Phil. 4:11-13.

Consistent Character

Inconsistency is one of the most glaring evidences of superficial faith. Numerous stories about ministers whose lives are inconsistent with the gospel message that they proclaim have been revealed. Small inconsistencies in ministry are like weeds in the lawn. Without attention, they grow into larger problems that affect the whole of ministry.

Failed ministries occur when ministers refuse to acknowledge the weeds growing in their lives. Anger, deception, laziness, or a lack of kindness are all red flags that something is wrong in a person's inner life. Untended, those behaviors will erode trust and lead to ministry failure.

The list of fruit the Holy Spirit produces in disciples of Christ provides a measure for consistent character. The result of consistently walking in the Spirit bears the fruit of *"love, joy, peace, patience, kindness, goodness, faithfulness, gentleness, and self-control."*[10] Developing habits that lead to walking in the Spirit is an essential practice for ministers who want to cultivate consistent character.

---

[9] This discussion is adapted from the *Younique Personal Vision Journey*, © Younique. Pg. 36.
[10] Galatians 5:22.

Numerous examples of ministers who have served with love, joy, faithfulness and humility also exist. Their lives demonstrate consistency, and when they fail in small things, they are quick to seek forgiveness. The spiritual fruit of their lives is evident for public inspection and it is often seen in the lives of others whom they have discipled and mentored. They may not be well-known outside of their local context, but they are also not hard to find. Consistent character serves to help them have a healthy relationship with God.

Ministers who continue to grow in faith as disciples of Jesus, who repeatedly trust and depend upon him, and who develop consistent character will have guard rails to protect their long-term ministry. To reinforce the guard rail of the inner spiritual life the following steps are recommended.

Steps To Take

Spiritual Disciplines
Pastors and staff members should serve as the "Chief Christ-followers" in a congregation. They cannot lead others to be growing disciples of Jesus if they cannot demonstrate growing discipleship in their own lives. Spiritual disciplines break down the patterns of sin in our lives and replace them with habits of righteousness.[11]

Ministers can fall into the trap of using the disciplines as tools of ministry. For example, Bible study is completely consumed by sermon preparation or prayer is completely overtaken by intercession. When ministers do this, their spiritual lives become engulfed by the successes and failures of daily ministry. In order to nurture their own souls, the disciplines must have a place in the minister's lives where they allow God's love and grace to wash over them remembering he loves us and wants

---

[11] Foster. Pg. 4.

to extend grace to us. They must take time to allow God to identify the brokenness in their own lives, experience his healing, and strengthen them to walk as disciples.

What would some of these patterns of discipleship look like? There are many ways to let the spiritual disciplines build healthy patterns. Here are a few ideas:

Prayer: Set aside time for allowing God to speak into your own life instead of speaking to him on behalf of others. Take a walk and ask God to examine your heart. Have you been honest, faithful, responsible, kind, and loving? Where has God blessed you? Where have you failed? What temptations are nagging you? In what areas is your life drifting? Ask God to build greater patterns of discipleship in your life.

Study: Spend time reading the Bible asking how it speaks to your life rather than only asking how you can teach it to others. Let Scripture shape your life as a disciple. What needs to be enhanced or changed in your life? How is the Spirit guiding you?

Simplicity: Slow down. Learn to embrace the things that serve your life's direction best and give up the things that don't. Remember that "No" is a complete sentence. You might be happier with less; less distractions, less responsibilities, or less stuff.

Service: Find ways to serve others outside of your official capacity as a minister. Serve in a way that does not call attention to yourself or your role but fulfills your calling as a disciple so that Jesus and the gospel get the credit.

Reasonable Accountability
Too many ministers live in isolation with no accountability for the use of their time, what they read or look at on a computer screen, their walk of discipleship, or their emotional health. It

is easy to fear that an accountability partner will just be another person looking for or pointing out where you fail.

But every minister needs at least one other person who can be trusted to be **FOR** him. In other words, an accountability is not just watching for his accountability partner to mess up, he is cheering for him to succeed in life and ministry. Give your partner permission to gracefully confront your blind spots and point out your life drifts, because you know he wants the best for you. An accountability partner will listen without judging and love without reservation.

This kind of accountability will keep a minister grounded when he gets too high and lift him up when he gets too low. Most of all, having this kind of relationship can save a minister from the darkness of isolation where sin can breed and the habits that lead to failure too easily grow causing a minister not to finish well.

The guard rail of the inner spiritual life is designed to protect the minister and his ministry.

Guard Rails

Resources

Spiritual Disciplines and Personal Discipleship:

Mike Breen: *Building a Discipleship Culture: How to Release a Missional Movement by Discipling People Like Jesus Did.* 3DM. 2011.

John Ortberg: *The Life You've Always Wanted: Spiritual Disciplines for Ordinary People.* Zondervan. 2015.

Dallas Willard: *The Divine Conspiracy: Rediscovering our Hidden Life in God.* Harper Collins. 2015

Richard Foster: *The Celebration of Discipline: The Path to Spiritual Growth.* HarperOne. 2018.

Francis Chan, Mark Beuving: *Multiply: Disciples Making Disciples.* David C Cook. 2012.

Faith Development:

Will Mancini: *Clarity Spiral: The 4 Break-Thru Practices to Find the One Thing You're Called to Do.* 2019

James Fowler: *Faith Development and Pastoral Care.* Fortress Press. 1987.

Seminars and workshops:

Younique Personal Vision Journey: A process of Gospel-centered life design. www.lifeyounique.com

re:Focus: a journey to refocus your ministry. Hearing God Retreats, an opportunity to unplug and reconnect with God. www.tarrantbaptist.org

7
What's Your Fit Bit?
The Value Of Physical Well-Being

By Bill Jones, D. Min., Ph.D.
Neches River Baptist Association

2018 was a year that I will never forget. In February I had a routine colonoscopy. My internal medicine doctor who performed the colonoscopy came out and informed me that I had colon cancer. He recommended a CT Scan in order to determine more about the tumor. The CT Scan discovered that I also had kidney cancer. The solution was to have 50% of my colon removed, followed up by chemo-therapy for six months and then have the tumor in my left kidney removed at the conclusion of the chemo. In addition, I also had to have back surgery on April 10, 2019 in order to repair a pinched sciatic nerve and do a fusion of my L4 and L5 vertebrae.

For 61 years of my life and I had never experienced any major physical problems. I had only missed one Sunday from preaching due to illness. I was faithful to do regular yearly exams and I was diligent in arising early every day and walking three miles before starting to work. Walking was a joyful time in exercising my physical body and a great time to be alone with the Lord.

Guard Rails

I have long believed and understood that both our bodies and souls are important in living the Christian life. We know that God created all humans with these two interconnected parts, and that the health or sickness of one can influence the health or sickness of the other. God made us and redeems us as whole persons, and it's a Christian distinctive to care about it all — not just the soul, but the soul and body.

As valuable as both parts are, the apostle Paul goes a step further to help us understand the priority of being healthy in his first letter to Timothy. Exhorting young Timothy to be *"a good servant of Christ Jesus,"* Paul writes, *"Train yourself for godliness; for while bodily training is of some value, godliness is of value in every way, as it holds promise for the present life and also for the life to come. The saying is trustworthy and deserving of full acceptance."*[1]

However, during my times of illness from the surgeries and the chemo, I was not able to do the physical exercise that I had been doing regularly. However, I am excited to say that in just another month I will be able to begin my daily routine of walking again.

My journey through illness has made me keenly aware that every minister needs some guardrails for their life so that they do not become disqualified for ministry for a period due to their health. I want to encourage every minister to establish some guard rails for their life in the areas of physical exercise and physical exams. I missed an entire year of ministry because my health would not allow me to do the work of ministry such as preaching, teaching, visiting, soul-winning, etc. One might say that my health disqualified me from ministry – for a period.

---

[1] 1 Timothy 4:7-9.

Dr. Ronnie Floyd, who served for several years as senior pastor of Cross Church in Arkansas and who now serves as President of SBC Executive Committee, shared an article in *ChurchLeaders.com* on October 21, 2018. The article was entitled, *"Pastor, Do You Exercise and Work on your Physical Fitness?"*[2]

In this thought-provoking article Dr. Floyd shares two reasons why he believes that exercise and fitness are important in his life.

First, taking care of our body is biblical...without question, spiritual fitness is much more important than physical fitness; however, they need to be friends and companions, not enemies and competitors. Life is about priorities and my #1 priority is my personal walk and devotion to Jesus Christ. Yet, this does not keep me from caring for my body.[3]

Secondly, Dr. Floyd states, "exercising our body is our spiritual service to God."[4]

Then, in his concluding thoughts, Dr. Floyd shares the following four benefits of exercise and fitness. We might call these the why of exercise.

Benefit #1: Exercise and fitness increases the probability of my body being in better shape, which in turn should give me a much greater ability to serve the Lord now and longer in life.

---

[2] www.christianpost.com/voice/pastors-do-you-exercise.html
[3] Ronnie Floyd, *"Pastor, Do You Exercise and Work on your Physical Fitness?"* www.churchleaders.com/pastors/pastor-articles/335842-pastor-do-you-exercise-and-work-on-your-physical-fitness.html. October 21, 2018.
[4] Ibid.

Benefit #2: Exercise and fitness provide me opportunities to grow in my personal faith, as I use this time daily to have others pour into my life. Technology permits me to listen to others teach me, preach to me, and mentor me on matters of life, ministry, and leadership while I exercise. Therefore, this is not just futile physical exercise to me, but more deeply and importantly, moments to practice and grow in godliness.

Benefit #3: Exercise and fitness greatly reduces my stress level. I am convinced that daily exercise and fitness helps me view life in a more positive manner, all because I am reducing stress.

Benefit #4: Exercise and fitness improves my attitude. Pastors deal with negativity daily. People pour their stuff upon us and when we do not take it to God in prayer and manage it personally, it affects our attitude negatively. Therefore, I promise you, exercise and fitness will greatly improve your attitude."[5]

Dr. Ronnie Floyd has long been a proponent and champion of great health. He once led his church in a biblical fast for forty days, teaching his church the importance of prayer and exercise.

While I do not have the same commitment to exercise of a Ronnie Floyd or of a good friend named Ray Stanfield who is in the gym five days a week and runs five miles three days a week, I do understand the importance of maintaining a healthy lifestyle.

I have personally discovered that there are some guardrails or disciplines that need to be established by every minister of Jesus Christ. These guardrails must become our non-negotiables of

---

[5] Ibid.

life. And the reality is, if we do not establish these guardrails then we may find ourselves becoming disqualified from some great ministry opportunities.

The following are important practices, disciplines, or guardrails that a pastor should practice in order to be healthy and effective in their ministry:

- Take Frequent Short Sabbaticals
- Sustain Your Personal Relationship with God
  - Pray
  - Worship
  - Read and Study the Bible for Personal Insight
- Maintain and Nourish Close Friendships
  - Develop and Sustain Peer Support
- Maintain an Active Relationship with an Accountability Partner
- Monitor Your Balance Between Work and Your Personal Life
- Be Plugged in to a Group of Peers
- Establish & Adjust Priorities Based on a Periodic Review of Your Values
- Set Clear Boundaries – Say "No" More Often
- Care for Your Body
  - Eat Nutritiously
  - Be Physically Active
  - Get Adequate Rest and Sleep
  - Receive Regular Physical Exams

This list is by no means exhaustive but is a great starting place for establishing some important guardrails.

Let me also hasten to say that I recently discovered a great place for getting help with strength training and balance exercises. I had to do some physical therapy on my knee and the rehab center at the local nursing home was awesome. They were not only willing to do my rehab but offered for me to come by often and do some training there. Several of the physical therapists even offered to spend time with me on their breaks and demonstrate new techniques for strength building at no charge.

Chad Ashby, pastor of College Street Baptist Church in Newberry S.C. makes this observation,

> For all believers, physical health is not about being able to post your exercise times on Facebook, having more attractive selfies, or impressing the ladies at church. It's about treating your body as a gift—a gift that God expects you to maximize for his Kingdom's sake.[6]

I love the three challenges that Dr. Ronnie Floyd shares in concluding his article entitled, *"Pastor Do You Exercise and Work on your Physical Fitness?"* He said, "Start now – do something. Get it done in the morning. Be consistent five days a week."[7]

During the distribution of the land to the children of Israel in the book of Joshua, it was Caleb who declared, *"And now, behold, I am this day eighty-five years old. I am still as strong today as I was in the day that Moses sent me; my strength now is as my strength was then, for war and for going and coming."[8]*

Every time I read this passage of Scripture, I find myself praying, "Lord, let this be true of me." And then I am reminded of the journey that Caleb has made through the wilderness and of the

---

[6] Chad Ashby, *4 Reasons Every Pastor Should Exercise,* https://ftc.co/blog/posts/4-reasons-every-pastor-should-exercise.
[7] Ronnie Floyd, *"Pastor, Do You Exercise and Work on your Physical Fitness?"* www.churchleaders.com/pastors/pastor-articles/335842-pastor-do-you-exercise-and-work-on-your-physical-fitness.html. October 21, 2018.
[8] Joshua 14:10b-11.

battles he has fought. The Bible does not give us all the specific detail, but I can almost venture that the miles were hard and the battles difficult. Caleb had remained strong through the exercise of walking and lifting and carrying and probably numerous other physical movements. He was also strong through the Lord.

In thinking about Caleb, I was reminded of the great John Wesley. He made many profound statements in his lifetime and most have been quoted by a myriad of individuals. That is true of this quote that I came across on the internet several years ago. What is profound to me is that John Wesley made this statement at the age of 78. He said, *"By God's blessing, I'm the same I was at 28, chiefly by constant exercise and preaching morning and evening."* [9]

If God permits me to live a long life, I would love to be able to make the same statements as Caleb of the Old Testament and the great preacher, John Wesley.

---

[9] Christian Quotes – 92 John Wesley Quotes. www.christianquotes.info/quotes-by-author/john-wesley-quotes.

Resources

ChurchLeaders (Free Resources for Pastors)
www.churchleaders.com/pastors/pastor-articles/334087-10-questions-to-assess-the-health-of-a-pastor-ron-edmondson.html.

Pastors.com
www.pastors.com/prayer-and-fasting-in-the-life-of-the-pastor.

Episcopal Health Ministries
www.episcopalhealthministries.org/blog/a-case-study-in-personal-health-ministry.

Resources for Pastors
www.pastoralcareinc.com/resources.

Crosswalk.com
www.crosswalk.com/church/pastors-or-leadership/healthy-pastors-healthy-churches-healthy-communities-1414457.html.

Fit for ministry: Addressing the crisis in clergy health
www.christiancentury.org/article/2012-10/fit-ministry.

My-Pastor.com (Pastoral Care for the Pastor)
www.my-pastor.com/pastoral-care.html.

❦

8
Are You Smarter Than A Fifth Grader?
The Value Of The Sabbath

By Gerry Lewis, D. Min.
Harvest Baptist Association

A television show by that name may have convinced quite a few of us that we were indeed NOT smarter than the fifth graders featured on that show!

Yes, it was humbling.

But, though the elementary whiz kids made us feel inferior about our intellect—or at least our memories from grade school—we can take heart. At least we're smarter than **God**.

Say what?

No, we would never say that out loud or even consciously acknowledge it, but our actions often tell another story. In fact, the habits and patterns of many pastors don't just **speak** loudly, they **scream**, "I know better!"

Perhaps there are many examples, but this chapter focuses on just one. I'm going to ask you one simple diagnostic question that will help you begin to evaluate what your habits and patterns are saying about whether or not you think you're smarter than God.

How do you Sabbath?

I heard that pause.

You can't do that!

As a Baptist with more than forty years of "church work" in my personal history, I can confess that my models, training, and education didn't give much attention to Sabbath, other than the **rules** emphasis.

Baptists know rules. In fact, we are often known **by** our rules. I've had friends over the years from other backgrounds who didn't know anything about Baptists except that we can't dance. I've always answered that our problem with dancing is not **theological**; it is a **rhythm** problem. We don't have any! I usually don't mention the actual conversation I had about thirty years ago with a longtime Baptist pastor who told me that a dancing foot and a praying knee can't be on the same leg. (Insert eye roll).

So, back to Sabbath.

*"Remember the sabbath day, to keep it holy. Six days you shall labor and do all your work, but the seventh day is a sabbath of the Lord your God; **in it you shall not do any work**, you or your son or your daughter, your male or your female servant or your cattle or your sojourner who stays with you. For in six days the Lord made the heavens and the earth, the sea and all that is in them, and rested on the seventh day; therefore the Lord blessed the sabbath day and made it holy"* (Exodus 20:8-11, NASB emphasis mine).

"In it you shall not do any work ..." That's the **rules** emphasis and that's the only part most people remember.

So, tell me this, Pastor: How's that working out for you on the average Sunday?

Yeah, we punted that idea a long time ago. If *remembering* or *honoring* the Sabbath day is about avoiding work on Sunday, most of our churches are are actually set up to cause people to sin—especially the church staff!

I could spend paragraphs talking about different rules, but that wouldn't help anyone with the guardrails necessary to navigate the concept of Sabbath. You see, my friend, Sabbath is not about **rules**; it is about **rhythms**. I don't mean the kind of rhythm that keeps those awkward Baptists from "cutting a rug," I mean the kind of rhythm that is like breathing or like a healthy heartbeat.

The rhythms of Eden

The Sabbath command in Exodus 20 references God's pattern established in creation. God worked for six days and then rested on the seventh. Simple enough, right? Work hard for six days and then take a break. Rest is a reward for a job well done.

But I want you to notice something in the Genesis account. There is a phrase that repeats throughout the days of creation: *"there was evening and there was morning ..."* (Genesis 1:5,7,13,19,23,31).

The Biblical concept of the flow of a day begins, not with arising to work, but with retiring to rest. The "rhythm of Eden" is rest before work. On the sixth day of creation, God creates man. The seventh day is a sabbath of rest for God, but it is also a sabbath of rest for man.

But did you notice—it was man's **first** day. Before he went to work in the garden, he experienced Sabbath. There was nothing for him to recover from. There was nothing that he had done that gained him the reward of rest.

Neither did God rest because He was tired nor reward Himself with a day off in recognition of a job well done. God established Sabbath in creation and commanded it through Moses as a necessary regular rhythm so that we would not forget to live in step with His grace and pace.

What's at stake here?

Here's the mistake that too many pastors make: they think they can be in step with the grace of God through spiritual rhythms and disciplines, while neglecting the pace God established for physical rhythms.

I don't know how to say this any more plainly—neglecting physical rhythms will inevitably lead to unhealthy emotional and spiritual rhythms. It's not simply a possibility. It's a guarantee. And pastors who are out of rhythm emotionally and spiritually do stupid stuff!

They make bad personal and ministry decisions. They isolate themselves from wise counsel and healthy support systems. They treat other people poorly. They can't hear God clearly. They perpetuate and encourage unhealthy patterns of living among their church members (Hello! Sabbath is not a "clergy" issue).

In short—as evidenced by their fight against the healthy rhythms God established in His word—they think they're smarter than God.

I tell every pastor that will listen about the importance of consistency in days off, family vacations, personal time with

God, continuing education and development, and not spending too much time in the office.

Throughout my years of vocational ministry, I have done those "break" things well. I've guarded my family time, I've been stubborn in my refusal to compromise on my Fridays off. I didn't miss my kids' activities when they were still at home. I've done all those things I advise pastors to do.

And I've nearly burned out twice.

You see, those things are good and important, but they don't adequately grasp the intent of Sabbath rhythms of rest.

Sabbath rest is not simply taking a break from regular work. Sabbath rest is resting **in God**. It is not avoiding work; it is ceasing from the obsessive need to be productive. It is refusing to measure ourselves by what we can accomplish. It is leaning in and embracing God's provision. It is finding satisfaction and contentment in His presence. It is enjoying and feasting on His goodness. It is focusing on **being His children** rather than **doing His business**. It is doing only what is life-giving and restorative.

And you can't wait until it fits into your schedule, or until you get these last couple of projects wrapped up, or until the new building is completed, or until you've saved up enough money.

You also can't wait until your church members notice how fried you are and tell you that you need to step away. Most of them won't notice that you are operating in unhealthy rhythms. They will only notice when you've started acting like a jerk (and then they won't be compassionate about it).

By and large, our culture worships accomplishment and pastors often wear exhaustion and busyness as a badge of honor. And our church culture has bought into the lie that this is Godly.

There are two questions that people ask me more than any others: "Are you working hard?" "Are you staying busy?"

Good people who love you will compliment you for all you do and tell their friends about their pastor who works so hard and is always there for everyone.

Let me be blunt. You are not Superman. You are not God. You are not the exception to the rule and you are not exempt from the consequences of failing to Sabbath. No one will put your guardrails in place for you and you don't get to blame anyone else if you drive your life into the ditch.

And it's not just about you. We reproduce what we are. Unhealthy leaders do not make healthy disciples. Leaders out of rhythm do not produce disciples who are in rhythm. Leaders who do not Sabbath well will contribute to unhealthy churches who do not Sabbath well.

Can you see how smart God really is? Can you see that Sabbath is a really good idea? Are you ready to rethink your approach to rest and work and return home to the rhythms of Eden?

Yes, you read that last sentence right. To return to the rhythms of Eden is to return home to the rhythms we were made for. It is the Created embracing the design of the Creator.

Practical steps to help you put your Sabbath guardrails in place

Hopefully I've convinced you by now of the absolute urgency of the Sabbath rest guardrail. But how do you do it in the real world of twenty-first century ministry? I want to take these last few paragraphs to give you some tips to help you process your thinking and prepare for your own return home.

Tip #1 - Choose a day that works for you and your family. A *rules* approach would say that Christians should Sabbath on

Sunday (or perhaps Saturday, if we want to be really rules-oriented). Most of the authors I have read have concluded that it is difficult for pastors to Sabbath on Sunday. It tends to be the hardest work day of the week! Not only do we have our preaching/teaching responsibilities, but we also try to cram in as many meetings as possible on that day because it is so difficult to get people to give up any additional time during the week. The scope of this chapter doesn't allow me to address the death-by-meeting problem, but I think we have created a monster with the schedule many of our churches are attempting to maintain. We say that pastors can't Sabbath on Sunday and we make it impossible for church members as well!

So what day should you Sabbath? The day that works best for you and your family. What day is best for you to cease from the need to be productive, to build your family's gratitude to God for all He has done, to do things that are life-giving and joy-bringing, and to be renewed by unplugging from normal routines? (Don't automatically discount Sunday. It may work for you.)

Tip #2 - If it doesn't get scheduled it doesn't happen. This is true of everything that is important. If we do not prioritize and schedule the things that are most important, they will be crowded out by things that seem urgent. Before you know it, you've gone for months without a Sabbath rest. Stress is rising. Gratitude is lagging. Fatigue is setting in. And all the while, we really, really intended to set aside some time. We just didn't prioritize it enough to put it on the calendar.

Tip #3 - You must unplug. Our smart phones, tablets, and computers are wonderful tools for effective connection and productivity, but they are some of our greatest enemies when it is time for Sabbath rest. The world will not spin off its axis if you go for a day without checking email or social media or exchanging text messages. I would even suggest that the more you use your phone for work, the more important it is to get as far away from it as possible on your Sabbath.

Listen to me, Pastor! You are important. You are valuable. You are NOT indispensable. Here's the truth: if someone really, really needs you and it is really, really an emergency, they will manage to find you. You don't need the distraction of keeping your phone handy "just in case." Do not allow what might happen (but probably won't) to keep your attention away from God and your family.

Here's a challenge: Pick a day of the week that seems best, prioritize it on the calendar, and commit to unplugging. Do it consistently for three months and then debrief it with your family. I'm confident you'll begin to see God's restoring work in you as you return to His intended rhythms.

Resources

Mark Buchanan, *The Rest of God: Restoring Your Soul by Restoring Sabbath*. Thomas Nelson. 2006.

Walter Brueggeman. *Sabbath as Resistance: Saying NO to the Culture of NOW*. Westminster John Knox Press. 2014.

Wayne Cordeiro. *Leading on Empty: Refilling Your Tank and Renewing Your Passion*. Bethany House. 2009.

Shelly Miller. *Rhythms of Rest: Finding the Spirit of Sabbath in a Busy World*. Bethany House. 2016.

Roy M. Oswald. *Clergy Self-Care: Finding a Balance for Effective Ministry*. Alban Institute. 1991.

A.J. Swoboda. *Subversive Sabbath: The Surprising Power of Rest in a Nonstop World*. Brazos Press. 2018.

Guard Rails

∞

9
What Means The Ring?
The Value Of Marital Fidelity

By Dale Hill, M. Div.
Burnett-Llano Baptist Association

*Above all else, guard your heart, for it is
the wellspring of life - Proverbs 4:23*

We don't guard worthless things. I take my garbage to the street every Wednesday night. It is picked up on Thursday morning. It sits on the sidewalk all night, completely unguarded. Why? Because it is worthless.

On the other hand, we don't think twice about guarding things we consider to be valuable. We commonly build fences in our backyards to guard our privacy, install surveillance cameras to guard our property, purchase cyber security systems to guard our identity, and instruct our children to guard their safety.

But what about guarding our marriage? What can you and I do to guard our marriages?" The Bible reminds us, *"Be of sober spirit, be on the alert. Your adversary, the devil prowls around like a roaring lion seeking someone to devour."* [1]

---

[1] 1 Peter 5:8.

In other words, the devil is looking for ways to cause you to fall. And if you think, "That will never happen to me" . . . look around. There are people from all walks of life whom we view as good and upstanding citizens that have fallen into the trap of adultery. They never thought *they* would be the unfaithful spouse, but they let down their guard and paid a great price.

If marriage is paramount over all things, except for our relationship with God, then I encourage you to determine now to establish strong guardrails for your marriage. I want to share some tips I have gathered from many "experts" and personal experience to help you to guard your marriage.

Lean Into What Matters Most

Marriage was born in the heart of Almighty God, for the pleasure and fulfillment of man, His highest creation. It stands to reason that only as we are rightly related to Him can our marriage be all it should be and can be. Marriage serves a far greater purpose than just to satisfy our personal needs.

In Ephesians 5:32, speaking of a man and woman becoming one flesh, Paul says: *"This is a profound mystery—but I am talking about Christ and the Church."* In this verse, Paul delivers the coup de grace, the final stroke and focal point of the epistle, which is tied thematically all the way back to the first chapter. Like an artist making a final stroke before revealing his masterpiece, Paul discloses the ultimate mystery behind God having made us male and female, and called into faithful, monogamous, heterosexual marriages. For those of us who are called to ministry this has one great implication. The reason we cannot please the Lord while failing as a spouse is because marriage is a reflection of our relationship with Christ.

_____

That means making sure that God is always the first priority in our lives, followed by our spouse, next comes our children, and after all these comes our careers and everything else.

When we read a statement like that and think about it, it seems so obviously true. However, when we are involved in ministry, sometimes it's easy to become lax about holy things. That carelessness can even affect our marriage.

Some of us, in our complacency, may have lost the fear of offending God in his infinite holiness. Without a weighty, life-directing, biblical fear of God, we're left with nothing more than situational consequences as a deterrent to self-destructive behavior. And our journey on the slippery slope toward unfaithfulness continues until, at last, we are exposed, then we wonder that we could have been so careless and blind to the danger. Unfortunately, we see this happen regularly with political leaders, professional celebrities and athletes, pastors and other people in the news.

We need to lean into what matters most!

The Bible adds that marriage is to be "honorable among all."[2] That means marriage is to be an honorable relationship for both husbands and wives. There is no place in God's plan for oppression, either on the part of the man or the woman, regardless of the culture or background from which we come.

Summary
- Love God with all your heart
- Love your spouse as your highest earthly responsibility and privilege
- Love your children and extended family
- Love your job and hobbies and sports and everything else

---

[2] Hebrews 13:4.

Cultivate The Habit Of Open Communication

Someone once said, "Communication is to love as blood is to the body." Take the blood out of the body and it dies. When the communication stops or becomes toxic, the marriage will suffer accordingly.

The open communication I'm talking about isn't just exchanging information; it's being open enough to explore your own feelings, hurts, joys, dreams and expectations, and to share those with your spouse. That means as a couple we have to get below the surface and address the real issues of daily life.

Communication is always easier when we are discussing something positive, but we must strive to be honest and have open communication even during difficult times. Whether you just got a great job offer or are dealing with a financial setback, open communication will make the expectations of each spouse clear and help each of you to accept reality when things fall short of those expectations.

Agree to make the big decisions, like how finances are handled, together. You won't be tempted to keep secrets from each other if you commit to making all of the important family decisions together. This is one of the best ways to develop trust and mutual respect as a couple. And remember, how we say something is just as important as what we say. Try to keep your words kind and constructive.

Developing open communication is not an easy factor to negotiate since men and women are different in this area. Research indicates that women have greater linguistic abilities than men. Simply stated, she talks more, and in more detail than he does! A woman typically expresses her feelings and thoughts far better than her husband and is often irritated by his reluctance to talk. Every knowledgeable marriage counselor will tell you that the inability or unwillingness of husbands to reveal their feelings is one of the chief complaints of wives.

Ccommunication is a learned skill — and it's often hard work. We have to make the time for meaningful conversations. Taking walks and going out for dinner are simple ways that keep the spark alive and create an atmosphere for deeper conversation.

Summary
- Learn the art of open communication
- Learn to share a wide spectrum of information, not just feelings
- Learn to be honest and positive, even when discussing difficult things

Make Sure You Know Your Boundaries

This may seem like overreach, but decide now, in a moment of strength, what you will never do in a moment of weakness. This is not legalism; it's wisdom. It's putting guardrails where they need to be—in front of the danger.

Putting boundaries around your heart guards it as sacred ground. Your heart is reserved only for God and your spouse. That having been said, most people realize that we are born as egotistical, self-centered creatures, with an amazing capacity to rationalize self-gratification.

We should not be surprised that maintaining boundaries is an important topic for marriage since the boundaries were ordained by God. We read, in the story of creation, that "the earth was formless and empty, darkness was over the face of the deep."[3] Then something very significant happened. God created

---

[3] Genesis 1:2.

boundaries! "Let there be an expanse in the midst of the waters, and let it separate the water from the waters."[4]

God created natural boundaries between the land and the water so the earth could function in a manner that supports life. We, too, need emotional, spiritual and physical boundaries so our lives can function in a healthy way.

Having healthy boundaries will help us:

- Be able to say *yes* to good things and say *no* to bad things
- Better understand how to make healthy decisions
- Take responsibility for our actions
- Know how to set limits on others' intrusions into our lives

There are innocent things you did as a single that would be inappropriate to do as a married man or woman, such as driving alone with or having a private meal with a coworker of the opposite sex. These aren't sinful activities in themselves, but there is no reason to do something that could easily lead to things which are sinful. Almost no affair happens overnight. Many times an affair begins innocently, or even in spite of the best of intentions; but, if you don't start it, it will never be a problem. Likewise, if I am never alone with a woman, I won't have an affair. It's that simple.

Nor is there anything sinful about having a friendly personality and enjoying the opportunity to meet new people. But a married man or woman must be more guarded especially when they travel alone or are experiencing a dry spell in their marriage. In face-to-face encounters, I would hope the ring on your finger helps remind you of your commitment. But in our day, don't assume that ring will necessarily deter the attentions of another person. Coaches, teachers, nurses, doctors and

---

[4] Genesis 1:6.

pastors: Beware of the trap of tenderness. It's real and often a precursor to emotional and possibly physical infidelity.

In our new social media culture attachments don't have to develop face-to-face anymore. Consider the following,

> A recent study has found a correlation between relationship health and Facebook use that may cause more people to want to switch off the computer and smartphone in favor of spending more time paying attention to their spouses.
>
> The study, published in the Journal of Cyberpsychology, Behavior and Social Networking, found that people who use Facebook more than once an hour are more likely to "experience Facebook–related conflict with their romantic partners." That conflict could then lead to a breakup or divorce. The study, conducted by Russell Clayton, a doctoral student in the University of Missouri School of Journalism, and his colleagues at the University of Hawaii at Hilo and St. Mary's University in San Antonio, surveyed 205 Facebook users aged 18 to 82. Of those surveyed, 79 percent reported being in a romantic relationship.
>
> Clayton hypothesized that more frequent social media use and monitoring of one's partner could lead to misunderstandings and feelings of jealousy. The study appears to have proved that hypothesis by noting a strong correlation between Facebook use and relationship stability. Clayton posited that, for most, the correlation probably stems from jealousy and arguments about past partners related to social media snooping. Of course, the study also found that social media makes it possible for users to reconnect with others, including past lovers, which could lead to emotional and physical cheating.
>
> Clayton's study is not the first of its kind. In 2012 Divorce-Online UK surveyed British divorce lawyers to determine if

there was an anecdotal connection between social media use and divorce. According to that survey, approximately one in three divorces resulted from social media-related disagreements. Similarly, a 2010 survey by the American Academy of Matrimonial Lawyers (AAML) found that four out of five lawyers used evidence derived from social networking sites in divorce cases, with Facebook leading the pack.[5]

Additionally, the driven, competitive type-A guys tend to push themselves hard in their work, but find it less convenient to take care of their souls and connect with their wives. Often, they find it unnecessary or even awkward to form transparent relationships with other Christian men. Exhaustion can cripple their ability to think and render them susceptible to pursuing illicit relaxation as a means of immediate release.

"Understand the tremendous capacity of every human being to deceive him or herself when not connected to God. Know that, once you start making excuses for wrong behavior, each excuse will sound more plausible. As a result, you will sink deeper and deeper into sin and ruin. Admit that you can't trust your own self apart from God. Make the decision to stay close to Him.[6]

Summary
- Establish boundaries before you need them
- Establish accountability with your spouse
- Establish margin in your life to refresh your spirit and your will to resist temptation

---

[5] www.hg.org/legal-articles/facebook-has-become-a-leading-cause-in-divorce-cases-27803.
[6] Jerry Jenkins. *Hedges: Loving Your Marriage Enough to Protect It*. Wheaton: Crossway. 2005.

Increase Your Investment At Home

Of all the abilities required to make a marriage successful, the best ability is availability. When you make time for each other, the relationship will naturally get stronger, and you will discover spending time together to be a good investment that will pay great dividends well into the future.

We have all seen married couples where there is little verbal interaction and the husband responds to the wife's questions with small grunts. Don't be that couple. Your conversations do not always have to be about big topics. Sitting together in the evening and talking and listening to each other shows her that one of your greatest pleasures is being with her and hearing what she has to say.

Think back to your dating days or your engagement period. Remember the hours you spent, on the phone or in person, talking with your future spouse. When dating, there was nothing you could not discuss with each other. In fact, you could not learn enough about every detail of each other's life. It was "open season" on all things personal and aspirational. You shared everything with each other.

Communicating was something we did so naturally then, but things changed. The focus shifted from each another to establishing a career, maintaining a home and raising children. Investing time in each other was slowly replaced by investing your time in almost everyone else.

Men use conversation to move information. Women use conversation to connect with others; but the goal of having meaningful conversation is to talk about things that keep you current about each other's personal development and deepen your understanding of your spouse. Strong marriages are built by spending time together, laughing together, playing together, and talking together.

Show your spouse the appreciation he/she deserves. Point out all the wonderful ways your wife adds to your life. And not only on special days. Express your gratitude for how well she manages the needs of everyone in the house; how well she takes care of herself all while having to tend to others; how thoughtful she is towards your parents. Stating your appreciation for the multitude of niceties your wife does every day will increase your emotional connection and make her feel special because you see her as valuable.

Your wife needs to feel that she is the most important person on the planet to you. She needs to know that you're the one who knows her best and loves her most. Learn her love language and speak to her heart. Spend enough time making her realize that you are not just saying words to check a "to do" box, but that you genuinely appreciate all she means to you.

With that said, you still need time for yourself. "Absence makes the heart grow fonder." How much time you spend together versus apart will vary from couple to couple and should be discussed openly and honestly to the satisfaction of each of you.

Summary
- Keep the home fires burning as a matter of first priority
- Keep an interest in how your spouse is developing on all levels
- Keep your calendar full of things to do together as a couple

Guard Rails

Resources

Nancy Andeson. *Avoiding the Greener Grass Syndrome: How to Grow Affair Proof Hedges Around Your Marriage*. Kregel Publications. 2014.

Henry Cloud and John Townsend. *Boundaries in Marriage*. Zondervan. 2009.

Jerry Jenkins. *Hedges: Loving Your Marriage Enough to Protect It*. Crossway. 2005.

Willard F. Harley, Jr. *His Needs, Her Needs*. Revell. 2011.

Emerson Eggerichs. *Love and Respect: The Love She Most Desires; The Respect He Desperately Needs*. Thomas Nelson. 2004.

Ellen Dean. *Marriage Trust Builders: A Practical and Biblical Guide for Strengthening and Restoring Trust in Marriage*. WestBow Press. 2018.

Jeff Iorg editor. *Ministry in the New Marriage Culture*. B&H Books. 2015.

Steve and Cindy Wright. *Seven Essentials To Grow Your Marriage*. Prevail Press. 2018.

Gary Chapman. *The 5 Love Languages*. Northfield Publishing. 2014.

Ron & Jody Zappia. *The Marriage Knot: 7 Choices that Keep Couples Together*. Moody Publishers. 2019.

Guard Rails

Guard Rails

⌘

10
Where's Your Heart?
The Value Of A Balanced Life

By Anson Nash M. S.
Corpus Christi Baptist Association

Just a brief background about me, Anson Nash. I grew up in a very spiritually committed family. We didn't just go to church, we lived it! My mother was the church organist and secretary, one uncle was the music director, another was the treasurer and my grandmother taught Sunday School.

I grew up praying, "Lord, please call me into full-time Christian service." When I was registering for my Junior year at the University of Corpus Christi, a Texas Baptist school, God spoke to me, not audibly, but clearly. "I want you in ministry all right, but not the way you think. I want you in public school ministry."

I yielded. God blessed. I had 34 years of "public school ministry" as a teacher and principal. But God in his goodness provided me with opportunities to serve 37 years as a bi-vocational associate pastor.

Superintendent Scott Elliff once told me, "You could run a business on the principles in Proverbs." I have listed, by category, those wise sayings that inform our financial decisions and attitudes in this footnote.[1]

He was my hero, brother Rich![2]

He was the pastor of First Baptist Church, Small Town, America. His son was my best friend. My mother was his secretary.

I had many of the heroes of that era. For example, I owned a prized Captain Midnight Ovaltine cup. I also possessed Captain Midnight's secret code ring that glowed in the dark and had a swiveling mirror covering the secret compartment. Also, I couldn't wait until I got home from school every day to watch the excitement of "it's a bird, it's a plane, no its Superman." He was out of that phone booth [ask your grandfather] in a flash with his skin-tight red cape and blue bodysuit with the big red "S" on the chest and a red flowing cape. [By the way, it was all black and white on my TV.] I loved Roy Rogers, Cisco Kid, Gene Autry, and the Lone Ranger as though they were friends of the family.

---

[1] Proverbs on **Wealth**: Proverbs 10:15, 13:8 and 18:11. Proverbs 14:20 and 19:4, 6-7. Proverbs 10:2, 11:4, 11:28, 13:11, 18:23, 20:17, 20:21, 21:5-6, 22:7, 28:8 and 28:20-22. Proverbs 23:4-5. **Poverty:** Proverbs 2:11, 6:6-11, 10:4, 13:18, 14:23, 20:13, 21:17, 23:21, 24:30-34, 28:8, 28:27, 28:19 and 30:14. **Generosity:** Proverbs 3:9-10, 11:17, 11:24-25, 14:21, and 19:17. **Greed:** Proverbs 1:19,15:27, 21:25-26, 23:6-8, 30:15-16,. **Conclusion:** Proverbs 14:31 and 22:2. — Taken from Copeland, Mark A, "Executable Outlines," 2016.
[2] Brother "Rich" was not his real name. Although he has been with the Lord for many years, because he was my hero, I do not desire to besmirch his reputation, but he is a great example of getting off the financial guard rails and the devastation that can cause.

Guard Rails

In the real world, I had uncles and strong Christian men at First Baptist Church who stood in the gap for my absentee dad. The Brotherhood [ask your grandfather] even took me in as a member at 17. There were times when I felt sorry for my friends who only had one father-figure in their lives. But Brother Rich stood above all of them to me, physically and relationally. He was a "neat" pastor. He was my first youth director, my first youth choir director and a very fun-loving kind of guy. We took trips together, made visits together and fished together. He was more than a pastor; he was a mentor.

Maybe one of the reasons I was drawn to him is that he possessed all the latest toys. He was the first driver to take me beyond the 100 mile-per-hour barrier on the highway. We were testing his brand new aero-dynamic Chrysler. He purchased an expensive set of golf clubs so he could further relationships with men in the church and community.

Brother Rich had come to us from a rural First Baptist Church where he had been forced to leave because of "political pressure from the Sheriff." [More about that later.] He was the pastor God sent to us to lead us into a new building program. As his contribution to the building fund, he furnished his office with beautiful furnishings purchased, on credit, from a deacon who owned the local furniture store. Turns out he owed a number of people in our small community.

That five- or six-year period created some great memories for me. I was so devastated when he left that I took my first solo road trip to visit him in his new home in Del Rio. His departure created some not so great memories for me also. He introduced me to the first floor fight I had witnessed in the church where I grew up. [Maybe God was preparing me even then to be a Director of Missions.]

It was ugly! Men who had taught me in Sunday School and mentored me in Brotherhood were now shouting at the pastor in a called business meeting. Tempers flared from these otherwise mild-mannered guys I knew and loved. I was oblivious at the time, maybe biased by my close relationship, maybe because I was left out of the loop as a teenager. I had no idea what the war was about. [As a side note, it was a tribute to my church-secretary-mom that I didn't know what was going on. She took confidentiality seriously. She never, ever brought home gossip or "prayer requests" regarding what happened in the office behind closed doors.]

That fateful business meeting ended with the pastor being physically chased out of the building. I was shocked! I was hurt! I was confused! As days and weeks passed and I began piecing things together, I found out what the "war" was all about. Seems that pastor Rich and a friend from the previous church had borrowed a significant amount of money for a chicken farm that went sour. They left that rural town owing a loan they could not repay. Turns out the "political pressure from the Sheriff" was more accurately a "run-in with the law." Failure to stay within his financial guard rails cost Pastor Rich his church, his respect, his family's peace and his witness.

Autobiographically, I want to share why I chose "financial health" as my guard rail. I started working for my grandfather's engineering company when I was in elementary school. I made more money than any of my friends. I always tithed the first .10 of every dollar. Then I saved the rest.

My goal was to become a millionaire by the age of 40. By age 44, 1984, I was nearly three-quarters there [assets = $716,000]. In today's dollars, I would have been a millionaire. We had inherited land and accumulated ten new rental houses. Because inflation was double-digit, our housing investments were doubling every year. I would go to my stock broker's office and watch the old men in their suspenders and bowties sitting all day watching the stock ticker on the wall.

Guard Rails

My dream was to retire early and manage my investments. Then a number of things began to happen to our financial kingdom. My wife is a great cook and thought it would be fun to own a restaurant. For us, buying a restaurant was a huge mistake! The work was killing my wife and we lost $50,000 on the business. Neither one of us knew how to run a restaurant.

The foundation of our house broke into five sections. Our daughter was in college sleeping on her apartment floor. We had no money to help her. When our car died on the side of the road, I called my mechanic and told him if he would pick it up, he could have it. Linda went for 18 months walking wherever she had to go. We couldn't even pay our car insurance.

The real estate market was collapsing. God was taking everything we had worked so hard to accumulate, one dollar at a time. I finally said, "God, can we just liquidate everything and write you one check?" I can tell you now, it was one of the best lesson's I've ever learned but the tuition was extremely high.

In the middle of all of this, I went on a hunting trip with a Christian businessman. This businessman had just gone through losing all of his money on a bad investment. He had lost everything, for himself and his clients—but he had a peace about it.

He knew that God was in charge of his life and he didn't have to understand why that happened. His story gave me such peace. Suddenly I knew why God sent me on that hunting trip! I learned that God and I had different agendas about money.

I learned that all God wanted from me was a love relationship.[3] He was not impressed by the size of my toys.

God doesn't care whether I'm rich or poor—He loves me just like I am. I surrendered everything to Him. I surrendered my dream of being a millionaire. I surrendered my dream of retiring and managing my investments. I said, "Lord, I'll do whatever you want, and I'll depend on you for whatever you want to give me." If I would have followed my millionaire dream, I would not be writing this to you today. I would not be serving as the Executive Director of the Corpus Christi Baptist Association. I would not have been the Small Group Pastor at Padre Island Baptist Church for the last 19 years. Instead, I would be serving myself, managing my investments and traveling.

Is it wrong to be rich? It was for me! God knows what we need and what we don't need. The Association sent me to a training event at Ridgecrest, North Carolina many years ago. The leader made a statement that taught me a life lesson. "It doesn't matter," he said, "who signs your paycheck, it doesn't matter what your job title is. The only thing that matters is that you are doing today what God wants you to do. He'll take care of the rest."[4]

God has continued to take care of the rest.

---

[3] Blackaby, Henry & Richard, and King, Claude. *Experiencing God: Knowing and Doing the Will of God, Revised and Expanded.* Broadman & Holman Books. 2008.

[4] I was the Associational Church Training/Discipleship Director. The leader of the breakout session referred to was taught by one of the Blackaby brothers. It's the only thing I remember from that week, but it was life changing.

Guard Rails

Steps To Put The Guard Rails In Place And Keep Them There

1. Prayer, fasting and Bible study. Pray through verses on money and finances [stewardship].

2. Put one-or-two year's income in savings or money market accounts. If you do this, you will not only avoid borrowing for emergencies, you will have money to catch the $100,000 deals for $50,000. It may take you four or five years to do this, but you can one day "live like nobody else."

3. Budget. As Dave Ramsey says, "Give every dollar a name." Otherwise, the money will slip through your fingers and you won't even know what happened.

4. Live substantially below your income. Anyone can spend more than they make. A few years ago we leased property to an oil company to drill a well. When the well came in, the first check allowed us to buy my wife a luxury sports convertible with cash. Our CPA warned us that he had seen many royalty owners adjust their lifestyles to meet their income only to find themselves in trouble four years later when the oil or gas well stopped producing. On the television show, McMillan and Wife, Sgt. Enright asked, "Commissioner, can you tell me how a man with a million dollars can go broke?" To which police Commissioner McMillan replied, "Spend a million-and-a-half."

5. Establish a habit of giving. Develop a spirit of generosity. We are blessed in order to be a blessing. In our city, the water department is constantly having to go to the fire hydrant at the end a waterline to let the water flow enough to keep the water from becoming stale. The same thing happens when we plug up one end of the blessings' pipeline that flows from our Father.

6. Teach your children to work, spend wisely, save and give. Your children are the greatest heritage you will leave. Leave them capable of living in financial peace.

7. Establish priorities. This is essentially what you do with a budget. It is true that you can look at a person's checkbook to know where his treasure is and look at his calendar to inspect his stewardship of time.

8. Develop a thankful attitude. If we live in an attitude of gratitude, people will see there is something different about us.

9. Reject a fearful spirit. Most hoarding is the offspring of fear of being without. We are afraid we will look unsuccessful. We are afraid we won't be able to pay the light bill if we pay the tithe this month. There is a concern that our money will run out before our month does, or our retirement fund will not outlast our retirement. I have a Christian friend who sells life insurance. His philosophy is that the last check you write should be to the funeral director…and that should bounce. His point being if you have insurance to cover your family after you are gone, you don't have to worry about money while you're alive.[5]

10. Forget about keeping up with the Jones's, they just refinanced! Find your balance between Asceticism and Materialism.

---

[5] Bill Bevill, First Baptist Church, Corpus Christi.

Guard Rails

Resources

Larry Burkett. *Principles Under Scrutiny*. Christian Financial Concepts: Dahoohego. 1990.

Richard Carlson. *Don't Sweat the Small Stuff*. New York: Hyperion. 1997.

George S. Clason. *The Richest Man in Babylon*. 1928.

Stephen Covey. *The Seven Habits of Highly Effective People*. New York: Fireside. 1989.

Lee Ann Crockett. *Preventing Fraud in Church Accounting*. San Antonio. 2018.

ECFA.com, Evangelical Council for Financial Accountability.

Faith and Finances: https://resources.seedbed.com/faith-and-finances

Leslie B. Flynn. *Your God and Your Gold*. Grand Rapids: Zondervan. 1973.

Jamieson & Jamieson. *Ministry & Money, A Practical Guide for Pastors*. Louisville: Westminster John Knox Resources. 2009.

Dave Ramsey. *Financial Peace Revisited*. Viking, 2003.

Guard Rails

❦

11
Where Are Our Guard Rails?
The Value Of Proper Boundaries

By Darrell Horn, D. Min.
San Antonio Baptist Association

The Last Question

We began in the first chapter with an introduction on why we chose to write this book. Up to this point, we have presented nine vital questions to guide us on our ministry journey. Yet, one last question remains.

We conclude our list of ten questions with one final challenge: **Where are our guard rails?** The wise counsel offered in this book will do us no good if we do not have proper boundaries in our lives. We can skim the contents of this book, but it would be to no avail if we do not act on what we read. We must be intentional to place and maintain those vital guard rails.

It is too easy these days to find a headline concerning Christian leaders who knew what the guards rails were but either did not have them in place or chose to ignore them. Unfortunately, because proper guard rails were not in place, they ran off the road and disqualified themselves from leadership. In the last few months, the national and local headlines have included suicide, night club escapades, broken marriage vows, unauthorized use of credit cards, lavish lifestyles, unseemly text messages, abusive language and behavior, denying the Christian Faith, as well as inappropriate behavior such as language and physical contact.

I recently was invited by a university professor to teach one evening in his class. The topic he gave me for the evening's focus was, "sexual abuse in the church." Unfortunately, as I prepared for the class, I very quickly created a list of no less than nine examples in which I had helped a local church during a difficult situation. If I had given the topic some additional thought, I would have created a much longer list. In each situation on that hall of shame, every Christian leader had crossed one or more very clearly marked boundaries. They destroyed not only their lives but the lives of their families as well as they hurt their local church body and the church's reputation in the community. The damage in each situation was severe.

Once again, I ask, "Where are our guard rails?" The consequences are devastating, when we consider the alternative of not having boundaries or ignoring the ones we do have. We must have proper guard rails in place if we truly want to complete the spiritual journey that God has given us.

Guard rails involve setting limits not only in our interactions with others but also in our personal behavior. It is vitally important to establish what is acceptable and what is not acceptable in our relationships with others.

Guard rails are God's standards in all areas of live which allow us to navigate in the correct lanes as we travel on our spiritual journey. While we are on this side of eternity, our lives face many difficulties, speed bumps, potholes, winding curves as well as other people driving in the wrong lanes. Such oncoming traffic establishes our need to have firm guard rails. Without guard rails, we run the risk of disqualifying ourselves from ministry by not staying in a path that leads to holy living.

When I was a child my dad tacked a small race track to the back of an old white painted door. We kept the racetrack under the bed when I wasn't playing with it. I remember laying on the floor next to him as we raced the cars around the track. At first, I had a difficult time learning to operate the hand controls to adjust the speed of the small electric cars. He typically won as our cars raced around the track because he could slow his car down to navigate the curves. Since we had no guard rails, my car would fly off the track when it rounded the curves. I remember the frustration I felt when I couldn't keep the car on the track. When we are not able to keep our lives on track, we experience frustration and then wonder why life is so difficult. Maybe we don't have the proper guard rails in place.

Living Without Guard Rails

On the last night of an international mission trip that Pastor Noel was leading with one member of his staff and several members of his congregation, he received a call from his wife on the hotel phone. Noel had left his personal phone at home during the trip and his wife Leona had looked through his text messages. She was calling because she wanted to know why the children's minister, who was a young married female, had been sending him so many graphic text messages. She also wanted to know who the other person was he had been texting at 2 a.m. in the morning when he should have been asleep next to her. He tried to deny everything, but it only made things worse. After the call, Noel quietly informed the children's minister, who was also on the trip, that their private intimate relationship had been discovered. Noel caught the earliest plane home the next morning leaving his staff member to do damage control.

On the flight Noel took some time to evaluate his life.

Up until this time Noel would have been considered a model leader in every area of life. Everything had been going well for him. All the seeds of his hard work over the past years had produced a fruitful harvest in his life. He was the poster child for success. He was a well-respected pastor, not only in his church and community, but also in the local Association of churches. He was looked upon as a leader among leaders.

Educationally, Noel had recently completed his Doctorate degree in counseling. He felt he was at the top of his game. His hard work and dedication had once again paid big dividends for him. He had already published several books and was working on several more to soon be released. One of the local radio stations began having him as a guest on a live broadcast. As a part of the format, Noel would counsel individuals 'live' on air when they called into the program. Such radio exposure even broadened his influence beyond his own community and into a larger geographical region.

In ministry, Noel had hit a nice stretch of open highway. He could see no roadblocks or major obstacles both in either the short-term or the long-term view. He had seen no reason for guard rails in his life. He felt he could put things on cruise control and coast for a while. The church, where he had become pastor just a few short years ago, was doing well. They recently voted to start a facility expansion project, which included a large fellowship hall and additional educational space. The total amount of giving by church members was up. Everyone was excited and satisfied with Noel's leadership.

On the home front, his wife and children were doing well. It had taken some time to adjust, but they now seemed to be happy and content in their new community. The last church where Noel had served as pastor was behind them. Even though there had been some troubled times, they were happy to have this new start. Noel's wife, Leona, was excited about the recent successes that he had experienced.

Guard Rails

Noel was active in his local Association of churches. He was well liked by other ministers and served as the leader of one of the Association priority teams. With leadership positions rotating each year, Noel was in line to quickly become the Vice-Moderator. After two years he could become the main leader in the Association, behind the Director, by serving as the Moderator.

Noel's influence was growing in all areas. He had seen no reason to have guard rails when everything seemed fine. There were no problems, no twists and turns in the road ahead. He could handle the added stress that success brings, he thought. Needing guard rails was a sign of weakness or lack of character he reasoned.

With such success as he was experiencing, his schedule had become so overloaded that he couldn't keep up with the demand. He began to cut corners in order to save time. He thought no one would notice if he didn't add the needed footnotes in the things he wrote and published. It wasn't really plagiarism if he intended to go back and provide the proper information later was it? Even when he preached, it wasn't a big deal that he downloaded his Sunday sermons from the internet. He didn't have the emotional energy to study and justified his choice because his time was limited. No one seemed to notice. Besides, he was gaining in influence. The harmless flirting with female waitresses or coarse jesting were only to relieve his stress. His wife understood that his job had increasing demands on his time. She was concerned for him being under such stress. She quietly endured the situation. The number of missed evening meals with the family increased. Then there was the financial pressure resulting from his overspending. The monthly payment on his new car was using all the extra cash in the family budget.

Noel assumed that the added success and demand on his schedule had created the added pressure to perform. He could handle it, he thought, but people began to notice that he seemed to be stressed all the time. He stopped making hospital visits and performing other normal pastoral duties. He stopped leading by serving and expected others to pick up the slack. His temper was increasingly harder to control each week. The pressure inside the emotional volcano was building. He had hoped this mission trip would provide the relaxation he felt he needed and deserved.

Then finally, things fell apart.

Before the plane could hit the ground back home, the sordid details had leaked out to the church elders by the team members calling home. The Elders quickly called the Director of the local Association of churches for help. Leona called the Director also and asked him to pick Noel up at the airport. The two men talked privately on the ride from the airport about the need for and process of restoration.

When Noel arrived home, he and Leona talked. It was then she realized that Noel's late nights studying at the church office were not really about sermon preparation at all but were actually the secret rendezvous of Noel and the children's minister in his office. The church members were devastated as the news leaked out to the whole congregation. The additional phone number, to which he had been sending text messages, was revealed to be an unmarried female in the church who had rejected his advances several times. He was seeking emotional and physical connection outside of his marriage. Thankfully she rejected all of his advances.

Was this the only area where Pastor Noel had fallen off his pedestal? In an ongoing discussion with the Director of the local Association of churches, the elders did some additional digging and discovered new information concerning the church loan for the new construction project. It seems that the funds from the loan, as well as bank statements and other important church papers, were missing.

Noel didn't like anyone pointing out his faults or setting boundaries on his actions. One evening when the elders sought to hold him accountable for his actions, Noel lost his temper, blurted out a string of F-bombs, and stormed out of the room. Instead of quickly firing Noel, the church elders wanted to provide a restoration plan through which he could come under their leadership for accountability, establish some healthy guard rails in multiple areas of his life, repair his marriage and family relationships, as well as repay the money he had stolen. They were offering a grace filled response to the terrible mess that he had created.

Finally Noel agreed to submit to a restoration plan. The plan was for Noel and the elders to make a public statement together. Noel would seek the forgiveness of the church and the elders would communicate the details of the restoration process to the congregation. The elders wanted the Director of the local Association of churches to be present to help answer questions and provide support for the process.

At the business meeting, Noel thanked the church for allowing him to be their pastor and expressed how much of a privilege it had been to serve them. The meeting started off well. Then Noel quickly announced that he was divorcing Leona. After he shared a few additional uncomfortable revelations, he walked out of the church sanctuary. The congregation was in shock and each day that passed brought more anger as the church members became aware of all the things their former pastor had done. Noel left the church and his family to pick up the broken pieces. Noel then left town and cut off all communication with everyone.

About six months later, the local Director of the Association of churches was surprised when he was contacted by a church from another state asking him to give a character reference for Noel. What an odd request given all that had happened. It seems Noel had moved on with his life and was seeking employment as the pastor of another church. The Director refused to give a reference for Noel and encouraged the requesting church to call his previous church to learn about Noel's character and the devastation he left behind.

Noel's life turned into a hurricane that destroyed everything in its path. Even if something was untouched directedly, it was still damaged indirectly. Noel destroyed his own life, as well as those of others, because he did not have the proper guard rails in place.

Guard rails? Who needs them? We all need them.

Unfortunately, elements of this story have occurred over and over again in the lives of Christian leaders. Directors of Associations of churches know these stories all too well. Directors see first-hand those leaders who are like Noel because Directors remain behind, after the damage is done, to help a church move forward.

Where are your guard rails?

Notable Quotes

"Boundaries are so important in every area of our lives. Without them, anarchy and chaos would have free reign."[1] Personal guard rails are the physical, emotional and mental limits we establish to protect ourselves from being manipulated, used, or violated by others.[2] Guard rails are also limits that we

---

[1] www.moneycrashers.com/personal-budget-planning-tips-financial-money-boundaries.

[2] www.essentiallifeskills.net/personalboundaries.html.

set for ourselves in order to not manipulate, use or violate someone else. Guard rails work in both directions.

General
"Healthy boundaries play an important role in every area of our lives. From financial boundaries to relationship boundaries, we must take necessary steps to set clear boundaries in order to take care of our own mental, physical and emotional health. Without healthy boundaries, we will find ourselves drained, exhausted and overwhelmed."[3]

Personal
"It would not be possible to enjoy healthy relationships without the existence of personal boundaries, or without our willingness to communicate them directly and honestly with others. We must recognize that each of us is a unique individual with distinct emotions, needs and preferences. This is equally true for our spouses, children and friends. To set personal boundaries means to preserve your integrity, take responsibility for who you are, and to take control of your life."[4]

Communication
"Firm boundaries, such as prohibiting inappropriate language or verbal abuse in the workplace, help keep the work environment pleasant and professional. Workers are encouraged to speak in a respectful manner that is not condescending or abusive. With clearly defined boundaries regarding communication, workers utilize the appropriate tone and language with one another, which improves workplace interactions."[5]

---

[3] www.financialsocialwork.com/blog/how-financial-boundaries-help-your-clients-create-sustainable-long-term-financial-behavioral-change.
[4] Ibid.
[5] www.smallbusiness.chron.com/benefits-boundaries-workplace-10748.html.

Roles
"Boundaries help individuals understand their limits in the workplace, which in turn, helps to maintain focus on individual tasks. With clearly defined boundaries, workers understand their assignments and who to report to for help. Boundaries allow the workplace to function adequately, even with limited supervision."[6]

Behavior
Guard rails "discourage inappropriate behavior by setting rules of conduct within the workplace. Codes of conduct define what behavior is appropriate on the job and what behavior is unacceptable."[7] For example, "boundaries establish standards regarding physical interactions, so workers do not touch one another inappropriately."[8]

One Final Thought

As Christian leaders, we need appropriate guard rails in our lives. We leave this final chapter question, "Where are our guard rails? as a life-long challenge to each of us. Paul encourages us with these words,

> *Therefore, since we have so great a cloud of witnesses surrounding us, let us also lay aside every encumbrance and the sin which so easily entangles us, and <u>let us run with endurance the race that is set before us,</u> fixing our eyes on Jesus, the author and perfecter of faith, who for the joy set before Him endured the cross, despising the shame, and has sat down at the right hand of the throne of God.*[9]

---

[6] Ibid.
[7] Ibid.
[8] Ibid.
[9] Hebrews 12:1-2.

Guard Rails

May God help us to be *"an example for the believers in speech, in conduct, in love, in faith and in purity."*[10]

May God help us to finish the journey well.

---

[10] 1 Timothy 4:12.

Resources

Building Better Boundaries. www.cloudfront.ualberta.ca/media/medicine/departments/anesthesiology/documents/workbookbuilding-better-boundariesfeb2011.pdf.

Bradley Davidson. *Drawing Effective Personal Boundaries* www.liveandworkonpurpose.com/files/Boundaries.pdf.

Setting Healthy Personal Boundaries. www.recoveryeducationnetwork.org/uploads/9/6/6/3/96633012/boundary_setting_tips__1_.pdf.

Boundary Exploration. A Supplemental Exercise. www.therapistaid.com/worksheets/boundaries-exploration-activity.pdf.

What Are Personal Boundaries. www.therapistaid.com/woorksheet/boundaries-psychoeducation-printout.pdf.

How to Create Personal Boundaries. www.uky.edu/hr/sites/www.uky.edu.hr/files/wellness/images/Conf14_Boundaries.pdf.

Guard Rails

ABOUT THE AUTHORS
Alphabetical Order

David Bowman has served as the Executive Director of the Tarrant Baptist Association located in Fort Worth, Texas since 2011. He earned a Doctor of Ministry degree in Preaching from the Southwestern Baptist Theological Seminary.

Tom Henderson has served as the Director of Missions of the Bell Baptist Association located in Temple, Texas since 2006. He earned a Doctor of Philosophy degree in Pastoral Care with a Missions minor from the Southwestern Baptist Theological Seminary.

Dale Hill has served as the Executive Director of the Burnet-Llano Baptist Association since 2018. He served as the Executive Director of the Galveston Baptist Association from 2014-2018. He earned a Master of Divinity degree from the Southwestern Baptist Theological Seminary. He has done Doctor of Ministry work at the Fuller Seminary and the Houston Graduate School of Theology.

Darrell Horn has served as the Executive Director of the San Antonio Baptist Association located in San Antonio, Texas since 2015. He served as the Executive Director for the San Felipe Baptist Association from 2004-2015. He earned a Doctor of Ministry degree in Missions and Evangelism from the Southwestern Baptist Theological Seminary.

Bill Jones has served as the Executive Director of the Neches River Baptist Association located in Crockett, Texas since 2005. He earned a Doctor of Ministry degree and a Doctor of Philosophy degree in Apologetics from the Louisiana Baptist Theological Seminary.

Gerry Lewis has served as the Executive Director/Lead Strategist of the Harvest Baptist Association located in Decatur, Texas since 2008. He earned a Doctor of Ministry degree in Discipleship from the Golden Gate Baptist Theological Seminary.

Ernie McCoulskey has served as the Executive Director of the Kauf Van Baptist Association located in Terrell, Texas since 2006. He earned a Master of Divinity degree from the Southwestern Baptist Theological Seminary.

Anson Nash has served as the Executive Director of the Corpus Christi Baptist Association located Corpus Christi, Texas since 2012. He earned a Master of Science degree in Elementary Administration and Government from the Texas A. & I. University.

John Thielepape has served as the Director of Missions for the Parker Baptist Association located in Weatherford, Texas since 2006. He earned a Doctor of Ministry degree in Christian Ethics and Pastoral Care from the Southwestern Baptist Theological Seminary.

Roger Yancey has served as the Executive Director of the Tryon-Evergreen Baptist Association located in Conroe, Texas since 2004. He earned a Doctor of Ministry degree in Missions from the Southwestern Baptist Theological Seminary.

ABOUT TXADOM

The Texas Association of Directors of Missions is made up of the Directors of local Baptist Associations of churches across the state of Texas. The Directors gather twice a year for the purpose of peer learning, personal development as leaders, fellowship, and mutual support. TXADOM provides a neutral place where leaders gather for learning and personal growth to take occur.

The Texas Association of Directors of Missions is committed to maximizing the value and work of Director of Missions and Associational Staffs as we invest in one another in assisting the churches of our Associations in Kingdom advancement.

www.txadom.net

TXADOM

Texas Associational Directors
of Missions Network

www.ingramcontent.com/pod-product-compliance
Lightning Source LLC
Chambersburg PA
CBHW060946040426
42445CB00011B/1024